HINDSIGHT

by

Bill Chambers

FIRST EDITION

UNIVERSITY EDITIONS, Inc.
59 Oak Lane, Spring Valley
Huntington, West Virginia 25704

Table of Contents

I Prologue 5

II The Planet Earth 6

III The Big Picture 19

IV Where Did We Come From? 34

V The Mind 54

VI The Body 64

VII Politics 72

VIII Why Are We Here and
Where Do We Go From Here? 78

IX God 90

X Odds and Ends 103

XI Epilogue 115

PROLOGUE

By the time you reach the age of sixty, you are a veteran in the human race. You can point out to your peers, and particularly the younger generation, some of the potholes on the highway of life. But who wants to listen—your peers would rather talk about golf and grandchildren, and the young folks just shake their heads and say, "What's that old duffer talking about?"

So all a person can do is to write a book about hindsight. Now you might think that hindsight is perfect 20/20 vision, but many people can look at something for 60 years and still not understand it. So nothing is guaranteed on this voyage, but it is difficult to believe that someone can read this book and not change their outlook on at least a few subjects.

Many fields of thought will be touched in the process of applying hindsight. Satire will be used on occasion to prove a point. Some will laugh and others rage when satire is directed at the twin taboo areas of politics and religion. So-called conventional wisdom and universally accepted theories will be examined. New approaches will be made to answer those three simple questions—where did we come from, why are we here, and where are we going?

If you are expecting a scholarly and well-documented tome, forget it! They say humans reach their mental peak at the age of 60, so the author has been over the hill for five years. Don't expect the names of books—if you get an author, you will be lucky. But isn't it really the thought that counts?

So, like Don Quixote, in the following chapters we will joust with the windmills of conventional wisdom—join the fray, or simply observe from the sidelines, and you may look at conventional ideas in a new light, after they have been burnished with hindsight.

THE PLANET EARTH

Matzel shifted the heavy bundle of food and clothing to his other shoulder and put his arm around his wife, Naca, to help her along the pathway winding thru the low hills up from the coastal plain below. A shiver shook his body as he looked over his shoulder and tried to sort out the happenings of the last few days.

Matzel was a fisherman. Daily, he and a relative had ventured forth on the great Western Sea to catch fish for the people in his coastal village. During the past week, the tides had grown increasingly strong and erratic. Even the surface of the ocean had seemed alive and agitated. Because of this, and because the fish seemed to have disappeared, they had come in early two days ago. They had pulled their boat up the usual spot on the beach, well above the highest tide. An hour later, they had watched helplessly as a giant freak wave had smashed their boat into the stone wall of a nearby house. Other boats and houses were also destroyed, causing a frantic search among the wreckage for missing relatives and belongings.

That night, a huge comet had appeared in the sky and the Earth had made loud groaning noises. Matzel had never heard or seen anything like that before. Yesterday afternoon, he and Naca had left the village and started walking towards the hills, where his parents tilled the soil. That was better than the destruction and fear in the coastal village.

They had walked steadily even after nightfall and saw the return of the comet—to Matzel, it looked larger and brighter than ever. Later, they tried to sleep but after only a few hours, a violent tremor in the Earth had awakened them and they had resumed their eastward trek. They had walked all morning and now trudged wearily thru the edge of the rolling hills.

Suddenly the Earth lurched beneath their feet, knocking them to the ground. Loud rumblings from the Earth filled the air. A wind began to blow with gale force from the West. As Matzel watched, a hillside to the north cracked open and dust and ashes blew out of a 200 yard long fissure. The entire Earth under Matzel's feet felt alive and moving, making it difficult for him to regain his footing. Lava started flowing from the newly created fissure and Matzel was dimly aware of other hillsides moving and breaking open.

Matzel turned towards the west and saw a sight that filled him with terror. Advancing across the coastal plain was a wall of water that appeared to be at least a mile high. It had already covered the coastal village 30 miles away and was moving towards them with incredible speed. The wind was blowing as Matzel had never seen it blow before. He looked around wildly for a place of refuge, barely able to stand up in the gale. He finally noticed the entrance to a cave in the hillside and, instinctively clutching his bundle, shouted to Naca and stumbled towards the opening.

After helping Naca with her bundle into the cave, Matzel turned in the cave entrance to take one last look outside. The wall of water now was scarcely two miles away and the sound of the leading edge of the wave crashing down on the coastal plain was deafening. The hillside around them was convulsed and dust, ashes, and lava were everywhere.

They scrambled blindly up the inclined arm of the cave and had just reached the end when the whole mountain side quaked as the wall of water crashed down on the entire area. Matzel felt a terrific pressure build up in his ears and lungs. As they crouched at the end of the cave, they could hear water boiling up the passageway almost to their feet.

With aching ears, heads, and lungs, Matzel and Naca listened to the water surging back and forth, and after a short time, finally drain away. Cautiously, they blindly groped their way to the cave entrance, and looked out on a sight that became vividly etched in their minds and was to be passed on for generations to come.

The scene was dimly lit by a garish pink light reflected from racing clouds of steam and ashes as well as flowing streams of lava running down the hillsides. The coastal plain was no more—driven down by the weight of the huge tidal wave, it was now covered by agitated, black-looking water. Giant clouds of steam bubbled out of the water, generated by submerged lava flows.

Turning inland, Matzel and Naca were amazed to see tall mountains, looming thru breaks in the gathering clouds, where only low rolling hills had been before. The Andes Mountains had been formed. Matzel looked at Naca and instinctively knew they were probably the only survivors of the coastal village.

The histories of all ancient civilizations describe similar cataclysms. First passed on by word of mouth, they were finally written down and became a vital page in each history. They all described waves overtopping the mountains and climbing into the sky. They recall cataclysms in which fire also played a major role. These cataclysms decimated the majority of each civilization, many times leaving only scattered handfuls, like Matzel and Naca. They were the fortunate few who happened to be at the right place at the right time. If the arm of their cave had sloped downward, Matzel and Naca would not have survived. Chance is the key word here.

And there was not just one cataclysm, as claimed by many for the Deluge of Noah's time. Many people wrote of four world ages ending with cataclysms. All the records also described months and years of gloom, when the sun could not shine thru the layers of volcanic ash and steam. It was a time of wandering, with entire clans, tribes, and even nations roaming the face of the Earth, looking for the sun and trying to survive.

The written records of every ancient people describe vividly the cataclysmic end of a world age. The Greeks, Egyptians, Hindus, Incas, Chinese, Aztecs, Mayans, Icelanders, Hebrews, and Arabs all have records portraying such events. Why is it that one will look in vain for mention of world-wide cataclysms in historical times in geological textbooks and other related fields? A review of the prevailing theory in geology is in order.

From the start of the French Revolution in 1789 until the Battle of Waterloo in 1815, Europe had been embroiled in bloody conflicts. After Waterloo, there was a universal longing for peace and stability. At that time, two theories vied for dominance in the field of Geology. A Frenchman, Georges Cuvier, argued convincingly for world-wide cataclysms occurring in recent times, but lost out because he could find no force on Earth strong enough to cause these cataclysms. Charles Lyell, an Englishman, with his theory of uniformitarianism, won the contest, stressing that for ages the only forces acting on Earth are the same forces we see today. Rain drops and wind wear down mountains a grain at a time and the silt is carried by rivers to the oceans, where the increased weight of the silt on the ocean floor gradually forces it down and causes the eroded hills on the continents to slowly rise. This, indeed, was true stability, just what everyone was looking for.

Lyell had to solve one problem before his theory could gain complete acceptance. He had to account for huge boulders found hundreds of miles from their place of origin. He did this by incorporating the glacial theory of Louis Agassiz, who contended much of the forming of the Earth's crust was due to continent-covering glaciers during the Ice Ages. These glaciers, growing during the cold periods, moved ponderously down river valleys and deposited boulders far from their point of origin, when the glaciers melted at the end of an Ice Age.

With Lyell's new theory complete, Mankind let out a sigh of relief. Our good old solid Earth had been changing only minutely each year for ages in the past and would keep on doing so in the future. The stars and the planets had been in their present paths all thru historical times and would probably continue on for ages to come.

This theory had a profound impact on many other fields. Astronomers were able to depict the heavens for centuries in the past—and deride the ancient astronomers as stupid and ignorant when their charts of the heavens in their times were at variance with the modern hindsight. Physicists scoffed at the ancient calendar of a 360 day year during the age immediately prior to our own 365 1/4 day year.

As for the universal descriptions of cataclysms in so many ancient records, Lyell had the answer; primitive people spent a great deal of time out of doors and therefore were very impressed by unusual natural happenings. A giant 50 foot tidal wave sweeping thru a low coastal village would look as though the wave reached the sky. Possibly the opposite might be true. An outdoor primitive people, accustomed to 25 foot waves, would not dwell too long on one 50 foot wave.

A case in point would be the biggest news to be recorded long ago in China, during the reign of Yahou. A vast inundation which overtopped the mountains fell on all of China. Many people were lost as the river basins were flooded. The survivors struggled for years to drain the basins, but in vain. The minister in charge of the operation, Kwan, after nine years of fruitless effort, was put to death. His son, Yu, finally succeeded in draining the basins and, for this service, was made emperor.

This was obviously no minor event—it was the main theme of all of the records of that period. In contrast, the Yellow River flood of 1887 killed one million people and an earthquake in 1662 killed three million people, yet these were treated as merely local events in Chinese history.

By now, even the reader must be asking why these ancient records have been so completely rejected. There are two reasons. The first is that uniformitarianism has been taught for generations and is the foundation stone in many fields. The second reason is that until the middle of the 20th century, no one had found a force powerful enough to accomplish what all the ancient records said had occurred.

In 1950, Immanuel Vielikovsky's *Worlds in Collision* explained what generated the force necessary for world-wide cataclysms, which had eluded both Cuvier and Lyell. Velikovsky postulated that the then marauding comet, Venus, made a close pass by the Earth, causing both a change in rotational speed of the Earth and a 180 degree flip in its axis, with the North and South Poles exchanging positions. Velikovsky further speculated that magnetism plays a major role in celestial physics, and that a giant electrical discharge between the Earth and Venus caused the polarity of the Earth to be reversed, resulting in the reversal of the Poles.

You can imagine how the book was received. The first publisher, MacMillan, had to stop printing it because of pressure from noted scientists. Scientists whose fathers had been weaned on Lyell were not about to be swayed by this upstart of an M.D., regardless of how logical he sounded. Their conduct prior to the space programs can be understood, but fly-bys and soft landings on the planets in question have borne out Velikovsky's assumptions, and disproved many of those 1950 conventional wisdoms.

As an example, in 1950 the best guess as to the temperature on the surface of the planet Venus was 63 degrees F and that there were no hydrocarbons in its atmosphere. Velikovsky said the temperature would be hot and the atmosphere would be rich in hydrocarbons. A space landing on the surface of Venus in the 1960s reported back a surface temperature of 800F and an atmosphere rich in hydrocarbons. Velikovsky further speculated that as a relatively new comet, thought by him to have been torn recently from the side of Jupiter, the heat of Venus would be internal and not dependent on the Sun. If so, the face of that slowly rotating body away from the Sun would be the same temperature as the side facing the Sun. This, also, proved to be true.

Pull out your 1950 encyclopedia and look up the planet Jupiter; a cold and icy mass, right! Velikovsky said it, too, was hot—as was later proved by a space probe.

To review some of Velikovsky's theories and see their impact on many of our ideas, start with his first premise; that many cataclysms have occurred in historical times. He believes two occurred in the 15th century B.C. and the last one in the 8th century B.C. The first was caused by the close approach of Venus to the Earth at the time of the Exodus of the Jews from Egypt. The biblical description of the ten plagues is a factual account of the effect of the Earth's entry into the tail of the comet Venus.

First a red dust, which turned the rivers to blood. Then a rain of stones, killing humans and animals alike, and even stripping grain from the stalks. The next plague was a rain of fire from the heavens. Currently, there are two theories on the origin of petroleum. One is organic and the other is inorganic, but both require ages of tremendous pressure, deep in the Earth, to produce oil. Velikovsky states that the tail of the comet Venus was primarily carbon and hydrogen gas, which burned when they came in contact with the oxygen in the Earth's atmosphere. Fire would flare up on a gigantic scale, and then die out when all the oxygen in the general area had been consumed. The gases would then liquefy and fall to Earth as a black, sticky rain, which was recorded world-wide. Much of it drained away underground but escaping gases from it reached the surface for many years. During the 40 years of the Jews wandering in the desert, there was constant mention of people being consumed by flames when they tried to start fires in confined places. Velikovsky believes that much of the Earth's petroleum reserves came from the tail of Venus when it was a comet.

As the Earth entered deeper into the comet's tail and closer to that body's gravitational pull, the rotational speed change and/or the reversal of the Poles occurred. This caused tremendous winds, earthquakes, and a darkness which blotted out the Sun. The Hebrew texts state that 49 out of every 50 Jews of the Exodus perished at this time.

As to the effects of the earthquakes on the first born (bkhor), Velikovsky believes chosen (bchor) was intended. The elite Egyptians, in large stone dwellings, died while the Jews, living in reed huts, were spared.

Velikovsky contends that after the first close approach of the comet Venus in mid 15th century, B.C., it continued circling the Sun in a very elliptical path which neared the Earth every 52 years. The second approach was almost as bad as the first time, again causing a world-wide cataclysm. Whether the Poles reversed again is uncertain. As can be expected, great fear was expressed by people all over the world when the next 52 year cycle approached—but Venus did not come close enough to cause any damage. But many people made human sacrifices and then rejoiced if the 52 year cycle ended without a cataclysm. The 52nd year was called a Jubilee Year.

Fear of the Jubilee Year gradually decreased as cycle after cycle went by with no troubles. But finally, about 747 B.C., it happened again. This time there was a new actor on the celestial stage; Venus passed close to Mars and drew that planet out of its normal orbit. Both Venus and Mars neared the Earth and the magnetic fields of all three interacted with each other. This battle in the sky was witnessed by everyone on Earth. The agitated tail of the comet, electrical discharges between two and possibly three of the worlds, the close proximity of the two bodies turning the dark of night into near daylight—all of this in conjunction with a devastating world-wide cataclysm on Earth would leave a vivid, traumatic impression around the world. From the Greek *Iliad*, the battle in the sky between Athene and Ares is a blow by blow account of the same struggle between the Roman Mars and Venus. In Mexico, it is the war between Quetzal-cohuatl and Huitzilopuchtli. In China, Venus ran off the zodiac and attacked the Wolf Star. Every people had their description of this encounter.

This last cataclysm had one beneficial result—Venus lost its tail and entered into a circular orbit around the Sun and became a planet. Before this time, a four visible planetary system was recognized but after the three world melee, five visible planets were noted, with Venus depicted as the newcomer.

Mention was made concerning the reversal of the North and South Poles of the Earth. Many people have this tradition. The Egyptians have one name for the sun that rises in the West and another for the one that rises in the East. And there can be no mistake about it being the same sun but called different names when rising or setting. Harakhte is the Egyptian name for the western sun—"Harakhte; he riseth in the West". And on a ceiling in the burial chamber of a pyramid of this reversed pole era, a chart of the heavens had been drawn, showing an upside down version of the *southern hemisphere* sky, exactly as it would have appeared from Egypt if the Poles of the Earth had been reversed.

Our current year of 365 1/4 days began after the cataclysm in the 8th century, according to Velikovsky. Prior to that time, a 360 day year was accurately used by the Egyptians, the Assyrians, and in the Veda period in India. Prior to the 15th century B.C., Velikovsky claims a year of even fewer days existed.

The second book by Velikovsky, *Earth in Upheaval*, uses stones and bones to prove cataclysms occurred in the recent past. He first describes, thru erosion rates of waterfalls and the mineral content of the landlocked lakes, that the last Ice Age probably occurred about the middle of the 8th century B.C. This is in direct conflict with the much earlier date proposed by most geologists. A look at why they back a much older date is in order.

Back in the 19th century, Lyell visited North America to determine when the end of the Ice Age occurred on this continent. He asked a long time resident of Niagara Falls how fast the Falls had been receding from Queenstown, on Lake Ontario. The answer of three feet a year he cut to one foot, as Lyell said natives tend to exaggerate. Multiplying the distance to Queenstown by one foot a year, he arrived at a figure of 35,000 years since the end of the Ice Age. A later check of the records showed that since 1764, the rate actually exceeded five feet per year. This would put the figure at less than 7000 years ago. Yet even this figure is highly suspect. When one thinks of the great increase in the erosion rate during the height of the glacial melt, the 7000 year figure would have to be sharply reduced.

Velikovsky developed what he called a working hypothesis; that tremendous heat was required to make the Polar Ice Cap and glaciers of the Ice Age. He contends that only an external force could cause a major change in the Earth's axis, which in turn would cause global volcanic activity. This would produce the two elements necessary for forming the Polar Ice Cap and the huge glaciers; heat to evaporate the water and ash dust to keep the Sun's rays from reaching the Earth. Under these conditions, vast amounts of water would evaporate near the lava flows on the land or under the ocean. The dust clouds would allow the vapor to turn to rain and later to snow, as the Earth cooled.

Velikovsky also reduced the role of glaciers in the formation of the Earth's surface. Much of what is now attributed to glacial movement was actually caused by huge tidal waves which swept the continents after the Earth shifted its axis. Erratic boulders are strewn about the Earth in a manner that would be impossible for glaciers to cause. In one case, a single mass of chalk stone in Sweden was transported an unknown distance (they can't figure out where the darn thing came from!). It is 3 miles long, 1000 feet wide, and up to 200 feet thick, and is quarried commercially.

Velikovsky makes an excellent starting point for investigation in any field. His approach, and the general reaction to most of the members of the scientific community to his approach, must be understood prior to any attempt to investigate in any field.

Velikovsky started with the "clean slate" idea. Anything is possible—let us correlate *all* the facts we can gather and see what picture develops. Today, too many people misconstrue the scientific approach into a method in which we build only on sacrosanct basic theories, usually of the founder of a field or his followers. Many of these basic theories were formulated when equipment and techniques for proving them were very primitive. Too often, when the equipment and techniques improve, the theory has become too firmly entrenched to allow an objective judgment to be made. Followers and apologists will support the theory thru any review and in too many cases, the theory will remain the dominant force in its field, in spite of strong proof to the contrary.

A major problem arises when a theory is taught in the schools as infallible—on this rock we will build our whole field of endeavor. Minds which used the classroom to absorb dogma rather than learn to evaluate, will spend the rest of their lives depending oftentimes false doctrines. For this reason, it is recommended that both sides of the Velikovsky argument be read, so the reader can determine for himself which side is true.

One tool that will be used on highly theoretical questions will be the psychic readings of Mark, a friend of the author. Mark was able to contact the Akashic and Cosmic records, which are the records of every act and thought of everyone who has ever lived on the Earth. Although Mark's readings in areas where conformation of his statements can be made is very accurate, in highly theoretical areas we can only use them as possible truths, with a grain of salt. A more detailed description of the readings will be given in a later chapter.

In order to check further into the question of how many years ago certain elevations occurred in South America, we asked Mark for readings about the ruins of Tiahunaca, located on the shores of Lake Titicaca. This ancient city, built out of huge quarried stone blocks which fitted together with precision, is situated on the shores of the lake lying between Peru and Bolivia. Altho maize will not grow at the lake's elevation of 12,500 feet, terraces for growing maize extend from the lake up the mountainside to the line of eternal snow at 18,400 feet. Carbon dating puts the ruins at about 4000 years old. The entire region must have elevated and/or extreme climatic changes occurred.

Referring to the construction of Tiahunaca, Mark's readings stated that the first section of the city was built just above the virgin forest. We will quote the reading directly. "There were two considerations. One was the increase in elevation due to vol—upheaval; the second being a climatic shift, this in the jet stream and a subsequent lowering of the freezing level at 17 degrees South. This a shift from 78 degrees south. This is not concentric to the Antarctic Circle, but crosses it, veers north and then returns south in a kidney-shaped pattern. The result, though not disastrous, froze the crops in the fields, virtually, and drove the people from the city."

We recognize that dates given in readings are not always correct, but Mark's teacher gave 2174 BDP (years before the death of the prophet-Jesus of Nazareth) as the last major elevation of the Andes and 2003 BDP as the end of the last Ice there. If this dating is correct, and it falls into the time period determined by the carbon-dating of the ruins, it would allow 171 years from the start of the cataclysm to the end of the Ice Age. 171 years for the following to take place—a change in the rotational speed and/or a reversal of the Poles, causing gigantic tidal waves, large scale elevations and subsidations, universal volcanic activity, dust, steam, rain, snow, Polar Ice Cap, glaciers, clearing skies, melting, floods, and a gradual return to normal, in that order.

Many of the changes were done in the first few days, or even hours, after the Earth shifted. The upthrusts and subsidations were caused by the miles high tidal waves which forced down the coastal plains and then raced around the globe, scouring, sowing erratics world-wide, and doing much of the work attributed to glaciers. It is almost impossible for us to conceive of the scale of activity during the first few days of a world-wide cataclysm.

Areas hundreds of miles square were elevated as the adjacent coastal plains were driven down. The top part of the compressing tidal wave would climb up the minutes old plateau and, filling natural basins as it went, roar down the back side of the newly-formed mountain chain. Sweeping almost all life away, breaking off trees at the ground or uprooting them, the tidal waves would race around the Earth.

Because of the rotational speed of the Earth, the oceans at the Equator are actually moving at the rate of over 1000 miles per hour. A reduction in the Earth's speed of rotation of only 5%, done suddenly by the gravitational pull of a close pass of another world, would send 50 MPH tidal waves surging eastward. If an even greater slowing occurred, the waves would also tend to move toward the Poles, as the diameter of the Earth is 7 miles greater thru the Equator than thru the Poles. When these waters finally met in the polar area, there would be a slowing as the waves ran into each other, which in turn would cause a great deal of debris to be deposited. And this can be seen today in all the lands of the far North. Debris hundreds of feet thick have been located in both Alaska and Siberia. This debris includes the remains of animals from all over the world. As described in *Earth in Upheaval*, "mammal remains are for the most part dismembered and disarticulated, even though some of the fragments yet retain, in their frozen state, portions of ligaments, skin, hair, flesh. Twisted and torn trees are piled in splintered masses." The frozen flesh, when thawed, has been fed to sled dogs. Mammoths have been found with semi-tropical vegetation between their teeth.

Because this meat is still edible, it appears that these huge animals were moved by tidal waves thousands of miles from where they were grazing in a matter of hours, deposited in a huge mound intermingled with tropical to arctic animal types, where they were frozen solid in sub zero weather. That is the only way the meat would not have putrefied.

Getting back to the first day of the cataclysm, we find steam and lava ash generated in huge quantities as the major elevations and subsidations occurred. Volcanic lava flows continued, heating the atmosphere and causing torrential rains. These rains added to the gigantic floods as the marine tidal water, trapped in inland basins, fought to get back to the oceans. This seaward flow, starting almost immediately after the original tidal waves, was once again incomprehensible to us in its magnitude. The majority of what is thought today to have taken tens of thousands of years to accomplish may have been wrought in a matter of weeks or even days.

As the volcanic activity diminished and the Earth cooled, the heavy rains turned to snow which built up to great depths, particularly towards the North Pole. As this was done under still dust-laden skies, little melting took place and the great weight of the snow converted the lower part into ice. The great weight of these glaciers caused them to move, slowly and ponderously, down river valleys, carving, grinding, and polishing as they went. As the dust finally started to settle and the Sun began to shine thru the gloom and melt the glaciers, vast amounts of water rushed down the river valleys.

By the end of the 171 years, the glaciers were much reduced in size and conditions were approaching normal. It must be realized that normal in 2003 BDP did not remotely reflect normal today. Large chains of volcanos continued their activity, altho on a local and reduced scale. Minor earthquakes occurred constantly as the Earth's crust continued to readjust. Comets were common, some so bright they were easily seen in the daytime. As Velikovsky points out, 57 earthquakes were reported in Rome in the year 219 B.C. We are residing on Mother Earth in one of her more gentle moods.

When comparing the dates given in the readings for both the last major elevation of the Andes (2174) and the end of the last Ice Age there (2003), they agree with carbon dating of the ruins at Titicana, but not with Velikovsky's theory of cataclysms in the 15th and 8th centuries B.C.; we are talking about different events.

We must also remember that when the Earth reverses its Poles, just how fast it flips has a great bearing on how much damage will occur. Also the position on the Earth of a particular country at the time of the flip can influence the severity of the damage; a country in the lee of an existing range of mountains might suffer minimum damage from a tidal wave.

Well, what do you think of Velikovsky's ideas about the recent history of our planet Earth? Fact or fiction? Can this M.D. be right and Lyell and the majority of the geologists be wrong? What weighs heavily in favor of Velikovsky are the written records from all over the world. Can literally thousands of records, written by hundreds of ancient historians, giving detailed accounts of cataclysmic events, all be in error? It does not make sense. It appears that Velikovsky could be right, and:

— ANCIENT CHRONICLERS DESCRIBING CATACLYSMS ARE CORRECT

— MODERN SCIENTISTS ARE WRONG IN THEIR DERISION OF ANCIENT CALENDARS WITH YEARS OF 360 YEARS

— PARTS OF THE ANDES WERE MERE FOOTHILLS LESS THAN 5000 YEARS AGO

— TIDAL WAVES SCOURED THE EARTH IN HISTORICAL TIMES, MINGLING THE BODIES OF ANIMALS ALL OVER THE EARTH, AND DUMPING THEM IN THE ARCTIC

— THE LAST ICE AGE OCCURRED ONLY A FEW THOUSAND YEARS AGO

THE BIG PICTURE

Now that a very solid subject has been studied, it is time to take a look at the other end of the spectrum. Have you ever wondered how we humans fit into the big picture? Were we all created by God in his own image or did we develop from a line of apes? Is our reason for being on this Earth more than simply survival and procreation? And when we die, do we go eternally to either Heaven or Hell, or is there some other life after death?

In order to expand the imagination to aid in grasping the scope of these questions, we will look in on an activity that could be taking place right now.

Oonap paused in his note-taking and turned to a figure manipulating the controls of a complex-looking console. "Switch on the unscrambler so we can listen to that radio. Where are we, by the way?"

Panna flipped a switch before replying, "Third galaxy, ninth orbit, seventh planet of the second quadrant, second sector."

They both turned and looked at a printout screen. Panna spoke, "Sounds like a sub-sonic air transport, but from the orbital satellites and debris, they probably have at least some interplanetary capability. They call themselves Earth—what a quaint name."

Oonap pointed to another screen. "From the large quantity of particulates, they are still relying on hydrocarbons for power. Move in with that scanner and we will take a closer look at this 'Earth'."

The large screen had been giving a view from about 1000 miles up was suddenly showing a rapidly moving picture about 50 feet above what appeared to be wheat fields. Oonap wrote "Wichita, Kansas," on his note pad and said, "Yes, definitely 5th plane humanoids with very primitive technology. And did you ever see so many canines? Yes; this would be an ideal planet to stud for that Quag Exercise."

Two other forms similarly clad in silver uniforms approached a little later, and after a brief tie-in, Oonap and Panna moved from the console area to a guard rail around a seemingly empty 15 foot diameter glass globe, which was bathed in a soft blue light. They leaned on the rail and looked at a long probe sticking out from the console, aimed at the globe.

Oonap spoke. "I still can't absorb the idea! Create a microscopic version of our system in order to study how other beings react to the stresses we are encountering in our Confederation. And then with the time accelerator, we can find out within days in the globe what would take centuries to discover in our system."

They moved thru a doorway down a hallway and looked out of a large window. Exotic flowers grew in black pumice soil while two bright moons beamed overhead in a dark yellow sky. Panna looked up at the sky thoughtfully and finally said, "Did it ever occur to you that our own Confederation might be located in an oversized fish bowl and someone else is monitoring us just the way we were checking out that place called Earth just a moment ago?"

He waved a limb at the yellow sky and continued, "And the lab is painted yellow—or wait a minute; maybe we are not being monitored at all. Maybe it is just a globe in a yellow living room of a house on the corner of 54th and Main, like that house we saw in Wichita."

Oonap laughed and replied, "You are out of your mind!"

You can laugh, too, but we do know that our Sun is one star among billions. As the astronomer Hoyle put it so aptly decades ago, "If there is only one chance in one million of another planet having the same optimum conditions to support human life as does our planet Earth, there would be a million such planets within range of our radio telescopes."

Can we find anyone conceited enough to believe that the plant and animal life on this planet is the only life in the whole Universe? With the millions of other possible sites, it does seem almost as narrow-minded as the ancient geocentric theory of the universe, with all the stars revolving around the Earth.

So the chances are overwhelming that life of some kind does exist on other planets in other parts of the Universe, but how advanced could it be? Could it be more advanced that members of the human race on Earth? When you think of a visitor from another world landing on this planet in the year 1890 instead of 1990, think of the difference in technology in just one century.

Now think of the possibilities of a planet which reached our 1990 level one million years ago. On the negative side, of course, is the real possibility of it being a lifeless, nuclear devastated rock.

In order to further explore the Wheres and Whys of the human niche in the big picture, satire will be used as a vehicle for opening the eyes of the reader, and the subject of the satire is, appropriately enough—vehicles.

In a small galaxy, orbiting around an insignificant star, is a planet whose inhabitants are having a love affair with vehicles. They are in these vehicles practically all the time, whether to go to the store for a carton of milk or joyride around the countryside on a nice spring day. Sometimes they travel on well-planned journeys while other times they seem to go around in aimless circles.

These inhabitants have a rowdy reputation when they are in their vehicles. Take very same and rational beings—the kind that help little old ladies across the street and attend church every Sunday. Get them behind the wheel of one of these vehicles and you wouldn't recognize them. Why, they will cut in and out of heavy traffic, yell at slower drivers to get off the road, and be obnoxious in every way. They always try to outdrag other drivers and even play the game of chicken to the point of destroying their own and other vehicles.

Among the closest inhabited planets, this "free-wheeling" planet has a very unsavory reputation and is given a wide berth. Few travelers dare show themselves on the planet for fear of being run over by the rampaging vehicles. Why, even the name they call themselves has a competitive ring to it—the human *race*! And their vehicles are called—human bodies!

Some of their neighbors keep asking questions—why are they always in their vehicles, racing around in circles and ramming into each other? Why are they so aggressive and competitive? Why must they always try to outdo each other? They even kid each other about what a rat race their life has become. Why don't they change their ways?

The neighbors asked around to find someone who knew about these characters. The only one they could find who claimed to have been on the planet was a funny oldtimer who talked so strangely they could hardly understand him. He claimed to be a race car fan, and he loved to talk about the mechanical vehicles called "cars" that they raced either around town or around an oval track down there. His description of the planet was given in this racing jargon, so it was awfully hard to tell when he was talking about the beings or about the so-called cars. Anyway, this is what he said.

"In order to understand how things work down there, you have to take a bird's-eye view of the whole circuit. Eons ago, the HEAD UMPIRE of the whole shebang was in a passel of trouble. Here he had billions of stars and planets and comets and things but it was as chaotic as could be. He had a few referees to help him but there was no ORDER—only DISORDER. So he came up with the BIG IDEA.

"He would send out about a zillion drivers, who would go out and survey and catalog the whole circuit, and also lay out racetracks on millions of planets to train these same drivers how to race so they could come back and help him run things. These racetracks would be rated as to their plane of difficulty, and each driver had to learn to race on one planet of each plane, starting at the easiest and working up to the most difficult. The driver had to pass a driving test before leaving each plane, and after completing the most difficult plane, would return to the head umpire and help him run things.

"It sounded great, so he did it—zap!—and at least a zillion of these drivers went out, buzzing around the circuit, counting stars and planets and comets and things, and also laying out racetracks. Now the HEAD UMPIRE also sent out a particle of himself with each driver, to sort of keep track of the progress of the driver and decide the sequence of lessons to be learned. But mainly the driver was to learn by doing. That was his entire reason for being there. This particle with each driver was called a navigator.

"The HEAD UMPIRE had figured about an eon to complete the survey, and it started out right on schedule, but a hitch developed. You see, when the HEAD UMPIRE made all these drivers, he made them like himself, and since he was perfect, the chips off the old block should be perfect, too. Young and inexperienced, but perfect. Every father believes that. But kids will be kids and these new drivers were no exception. Some of them landed on developing fifth plane planets and found crude lifeforms running around and that's when the BIG IDEA hit a snag.

"You must remember that these drivers were pure spirit, with no physical attributes. If one of them wanted to make a survey from the top of Mt. Everest, he just willed himself there and he was there! But when some venturesome driver willed himself inside one of these lifeforms, it sure revolutionized things around the whole circuit. While he was inside, he found that he could hook himself into the brain circuitry of the lifeform and assume control!

"Boy, did he have a ball! He ran that lifeform up and down the beach just like a jockey riding a horse. And he found that hooking himself into the lifeform's sensory system was fantastic! He had never sensed anything before and to run up and down the beach and *feel* the warm sand underfoot, *hear* the cry of the sea gulls, *smell* the orange blossoms, *see* the beautiful sunset, *taste* the sweet grapes, and wow!—every time he looked at that particular lifeform over there, he got the darndest urge!

"Well, when this pioneering driver got on his CB and told the other drivers what he had gotten into, the clatter of surveying instruments hitting the grounds was thunderous. All of the drivers willed themselves into lifeforms and raced each other up and down the beach. A driver would run a lifeform around until its tongue was hanging out, then will himself into another lifeform and race around some more. The drivers quickly learned how to take care of that darn urge when they were inside a lifeform and looked at certain other lifeforms. When the drivers were inside the lifeforms doing all of this, they were too busy to hear the whisper of their little navigators, urging them to get back to work.

"Later, the HEAD UMPIRE looked at his Timex and let out a howl. One eon gone by and the survey complete except on fifth plane planets. And the drivers there paying no attention to surveying and laying out racetracks, but instead were spending most of their time running around in those crude lifeforms. And golly!—do you see what those two over there are doing! Well, that does it! If you like running around in those gadgets so much, so be it! From now on, each one of you fifth plane drivers will be imprisoned in a lifeform for the lifetime of the lifeform and will repeat the cycle in other lifeforms until you get back on the

RIGHT PATH."

The oldtimer slapped a thin knee with his bony hand. "Boy—did the fifth plane drivers moan and groan! It was one thing to be able to will yourself into and out of a lifeform whenever and wherever you wanted, but trapped inside one for its lifetime—no way! It was fun diving a lifeform into that nice cool Minnesota lake in the summer, but to live there the whole winter, and only deerskins for clothes—no way! It is a little like horseback riding; fun if you do it at the time and place of your choice, but real work if you *have* to do it. Why, think of being inside that contraption *all* the time. If you want to go somewhere, one foot in front of the other, inhale and exhale, watch out for rattlesnakes, and here is a river; how do I swim? And hey, it's cold—what do I do for clothes? And of course, the never-ending struggle to find fuel for the lifeform three times a day—No Way!!

"The HEAD UMPIRE's CB flooded with calls from referees, who were getting calls from drivers trapped in the lifeforms, begging him to get them out. But he wouldn't budge. 'You guys got yourselves into those gadgets; so get yourselves out. Oh, I could start a welfare program, ADD; that is Aid to Delinquent Drivers. But if I did this at every rocky turn in the road, it would have the same effect as all welfare, and I would get a bunch of wimps back at the end of the circuit that would be of no help to me at all. I want graduate drivers who can choose the RIGHT PATH in all kinds of situations and drive in HARMONY with their fellow drivers.

But he knew he had a problem so he thought and thought for a long time, and finally had another BIG IDEA. 'Ok, you guys trapped inside those vehicles. I will do one thing for you. If you are going to be inside one of those contraptions its every waking minute, you will be so busy pushing the levers and cranking the wheel that you will have no time at all to think about the RIGHT PATH and HARMONY. So, in this fifth plane only, I will let each navigator create an assistant for each driver; it will be a CB operator, to rely information between the driver and the navigator, and keep track of other drivers on the course.' It's too bad; before he got stuck inside the lifeform, the driver could hear the whisper of the navigator, if he really needed him."

The oldtimer winked, leaned forward, and spoke in a lowered tone. "I'm a fifth plane type myself, in between heats down below, and like fifth planers everywhere, some of us believe one way and some another. Some of us believe these fifth plane drivers willed themselves into those lifeforms so much that they *forgot* how to get themselves out again—that the HEAD UMPIRE had nothing to do with it at all.

"Well, whichever way, these fifth plane drivers are trapped inside the vehicles, each with a crew of two. It looks like it should be a well-organized team. The driver, seated on the left-hand side behind the wheel, devotes every CONSCIOUS moment to the major task of keeping the vehicle on the RIGHT PATH. The CB operator, seated next to the driver, passes messages back and forth between the navigator and the driver and with his CB, and has a SUBCONSCIOUS knack of knowing what other drivers are thinking and doing. He is also the backup driver, as the driver has been known to freeze in tight situations and the little CB operator, as emotional and juvenile as he is, has grabbed the wheel and saved the vehicle.

"Now, the navigator sits next to the CB operator and on the right hand side, where he keeps a close eye on the RIGHT HAND PATH. He has AM-FM radio, police band, and even a color TV with satellite dish on the roof. He has contact with not only all the other crews but also the track referees and, some say, even with the District Umpire. With all this, plus a new crew member, he was a sort of a SUPER-CONSCIOUSNESS, and everyone thought great progress would be made in getting the crews out of the vehicles.

"But try as each navigator did to keep his driver and CB operator concentrating on the RIGHT PATH and HARMONY, things continued to deteriorate. The CB operator started turning up the volume on his CB while tuned to wild, rhythmic music called rock and roll, which excited the senses. The driver found that he enjoyed racing with his window rolled down in order to feel the wind in his face, smell the flowers, watch the sunsets, and regrettably, yell at the other drivers.

"Because of the loud music, the driver shouting, and the outside road and wind noise, communication was reduced to a minimum. Increasingly, it was the driver who ran the show, and he was so busy cranking the wheel, yelling at the other drivers, and enjoying the physical aspects of the planet that the vehicle got off the RIGHT PATH and wandered all over the course.

"It is a shame—the navigator sitting there with all the data to get back on course, but the driver never listens or asks. Well sometimes, usually on Sundays, some drivers go to their driving schools and go thru a ritual of trying to get in touch with the HEAD UMPIRE, when it is really their own navigator they should be trying to reach. But the CB operator knows it is just a ritual and pays no attention. On rare occasions, when the driver really wants to contact the navigator, and demonstrates his desire by fasting and rolling up his window to shut out the outside physical world, the CB operator has been known to pass information between the two."

The oldtimer impatiently snapped his fingers. "Hey, I forgot to tell you about the vehicles themselves. There are five basic designs, all very similar in construction and function. Oh, one is a little sturdier and more primitive, another has slanted headlights, and another is thought by its drivers to have a better on-board computer. But they all serve their primary purpose equally well; as vehicles for the drivers to interaction with other drivers. The fact that the five designs are named after colors—white, black, brown, red, and yellow—is immaterial. The vehicle's color has nothing to do with how the driver performs. In fact, drivers can draw a different color for each heat. And if a driver develops a hatred for a particular color, sure as shootin' he will draw that color to drive in the next heat. Remember; color, cubic inch, size, and even speed and condition are all unimportant. What is important is HOW THE DRIVER USES WHAT HE HAS in his interaction with the other drivers."

The oldtimer shrugged. "Now, you might want to know how a crew changes from an old vehicle into a new one. When a vehicle gets so smashed up or worn out that it can't run, it is scrapped, either by burying it in the ground or burning it up. The crew ALWAYS leaves the vehicle and goes to a rest area. On this planet you are interested in, the rest area is considered by many to be quite a heavenly place. Well, someone always meets each crew as they leave the old vehicle, leading them thru a gate to the rest area. A funny thing about this rest area is that it has many gates, each one leading to its own transition area. I am a volunteer at this pearly-colored one we are in front of now. Hey, we are in luck—here comes my boss. His name is Pete and he is showing an intergalactic tour group around and if we listen in, you can get the straight scoop on how things are done up here. But I have to warn you; Pete is also an avid racing fan."

Pete was an imposing old man with a long white robe and a long white beard to match. He had piercing blue eyes and his fingers gestured as he spoke. "When a race crew loses their old jalopy, it can be a traumatic experience. As we meet them at the gate, many drivers and particularly the CB operators are crying and afraid, missing their vehicle and other race crews still down below. So we try to ease the transition by making each area look like what they had been taught to expect, when the old vehicle gives up the ghost, so to speak."

Pete chuckled at his witticism and continued, "One group comes up expecting scimitars, dancing girls, and a land of milk and honey. That would be thru Gate 3. Another group worries that they will be shoveling coal into a furnace forever; that is one hell of task and that would be Gate 2. I am in charge of this gate, which is No. 7, where they expect harps and wings and clouds, so we give them harps, wings, and clouds."

Pete paused, scratching his beard for a moment. "The transition area is vital at this gate, because they are taught down below that they race in only one heat and then spend the rest of eternity in the area. It takes a while for them to realize that this is just an R and R, and they will go back down below to race in other heats.

"While they are in this transition area, the driver and particularly the CB operator can will themselves back down to the old racetrack and look up old friends still racing, but it can be very frustrating, as they can almost never communicate with them. The time period varies from crew to crew, but gradually the pull of the vehicle and friends below lessens and at last the navigator and driver leave the transition area and go to the staging area. The CB operator, emotionally tied to the last heat, keeps going back down to the planet, but finally just wastes away."

Pete frowned and scratched his beard some more. "I will never get accustomed to a beard. This group expects to be met by St. Peter at the Pearly Gates, so I have to will myself into this body, this robe, and this beard—and scratch."

He continued. "If R and R means rest and recreation down below, it must mean release and review up here. The crews stay in the transition area until they have released their emotional ties with friends and the old vehicle down below, and then move into the staging area, where they review and incorporate the driver's experiences in the last heat into the *Driver's Log*, which is the record of the driver's experiences in all the heats on all the planes he has ever raced. The new updated log will alter the driver's opinion on many subjects. It's odd, but the driver never even sees the log up here; and it is the navigator who updates it.

"After the log is updated, the navigator must make some critical decisions. He reviews the updated log, checking for the driver's weak points, to determine what experience or interaction with some other driver would most improve his driver's racing ability. If it is necessary, he can go to the track referees or other beings for help.

"Let's take an example; our driver and a wild-eyed driver in an old pickup had yelled at each other, smashed into one another, and really hated each other. Now, both of their navigators KNOW the two requirements for a driver to graduate from the fifth plane and get himself out of those confounded gadgets—GET BACK ON AND STAY ON THE RIGHT PATH AND DRIVE IN HARMONY WITH THE OTHER DRIVERS.

"So when the two navigators decide the hatred between the two drivers is the weakest link in both driver's logs, they get a racing sheet to look at future heats and try to find two vehicles in which to 'try it again'. By studying the racing sheets, they find, in Heat 429A, a vehicle TOY1033A for our driver, with a windshield so pitted and glazed the driver can hardly see the road. In the same heat, they find a GM8795B for old 'wild-eyed', with a motor that will hardly run. In Heat 429A, they will be paired, one pushing and the other steering.

The navigators, their main staging area task done, have one last cup of nectar and hold up their crossed fingers. One say, 'Sure hope each depending on the other, one pushing while the other steers, will get them to work in harmony. If not, we will have to figure out something new and try it again—and keep on running them around the track until they finally learn'. Then they take a few seminars until Heat 429A, when they wake up their drivers, create new CB operators, climb into the new

28

vehicles, and try again."

Pete now tries to keep from smiling but he couldn't keep the twinkle out of his eyes. "This pairing up of two vehicles is quite common. It has proven the best way to work on weak links in racing logs—pair them up so they HAVE to work together. Usually a tough burly pickup will pair up with a sexy little sports car, good in the fast lane. There is another advantage in pairing; the only way a new vehicle can enter a heat is to be sponsored by a pair. In that way, the paired drivers can explain to the new driver all about the dangers of speed and the new fuel additives. Some paired drivers tend to overdo it, telling the new driver exactly when to shift and where to turn. But they should remember that the new driver is working on his own log and it is best for them to show the way by example and let the new driver drive his own race. After all, isn't that why he is down there?"

The oldtimer turned to his listeners as Pete finished his tour and walked away. A question was asked of him, and he replied, "I am asked that question a lot, about why this planet is so rambunctious. Fifth plane worlds are a wild bunch, where the drivers are thought to have less outside control and more free will than just about any other plane. That's why it is considered by some to be sort of a penal colony—really one hell of a place. That's why it looks so much like a demolition derby; vehicles smashing into each other, sort of rubbing off the rough edges until they get well-rounded enough to go on to the sixth plane."

The oldtimer thought for a moment, resting his chin in his hand. He looked a little like the statue of 'The Thinker', except for his wings. "Besides the driver trying to reach the navigator thru that nit-wit of a CB operator, there is one other type of aid for the driver. There are several racing manuals he can use.

"These manuals are usually written about a driver who had graduated from the fifth plane but who had elected to return in order to show the drivers here about HARMONY and the RIGHT PATH. Now these returnees had a few advantages over the run-of-the-mill fifth plane drivers. In the sixth plane, they had learned a stunt or two *guaranteed* to get the attention of every fifth plane driver. Why, they could fix a flat tire by just laying their hand on the casing. They could run their hand over a pitted and opaque windshield and it would be as good as new.

Believe it or not, they could even restart a worn out engine that the best fifth plane mechanic would swear would never run again.

"Well, every few centuries, one of these returnees would come back down, climb into a vehicle and show off his stunts to gather a crowd, and then hit them with the message—the straight scoop on how to get on the RIGHT PATH and drive in HARMONY. It was truly impressive. Some drivers not standing around with their mouths hanging open would write down what they had seen and heard and someone finally stapled these sheets together. Then someone, usually after the returnee's heat was over, would scratch his head and decide which sheets to include in a new racing manual. Over the centuries, 2 or 3 of these manuals have stood the test of time and grown in popularity with the drivers.

"Then a school would be formed to teach the new manual. Well, at first it wasn't really a school but just a bunch of drivers sitting around talking about the great things they had seen and heard. Gradually it became more formal; some of the drivers would become full time teachers as well as taking the responsibility for copying, translating, and revising the manual."

The oldtimer paused, shook his head, and sighed. "These schools are a mixed bag. As the old saying goes, there is good news and there is bad news. Take one of the biggest ones in operation, built on the racing manual of one of the more recent returnees. The good news is that this school has an excellent record of teaching drivers how to drive in HARMONY with their fellow drivers. It's right there in the manual—'Love thy neighbor as thyself—do unto others as you would have them do unto you'. And by having a school where they can meet other drivers learning how to drive in HARMONY, they would all advance, sort of in a team effort. The school also reaches many drivers who would never think of the RIGHT PATH if left to themselves.

"Now for the bad news. Because of the fierce competition between the different schools to attract drivers, our school had a big meeting a few centuries after the returnee had left. The object of the meeting was to revise the manual to strengthen the sales pitch. They hit on a brilliant idea—use the fear factor! 'You have got to get it all together in this lifetime because this is it!

After this lifetime, you will spend eternity either burning in Hell or basking in Heaven, and only us teachers have the smarts to interpret the manual and make sure you get into Heaven. Only one lifetime, so you had better depend on us.'

"Boy, did that do the trick! Drivers rolled in, huge schools were built, more teachers were trained, and more tuition charged. But were most of these drivers finding the RIGHT PATH? The HEAD UMPIRE wants reliable decision-making helpers and not beings dependent on their teachers. The best pupil, from the school's standpoint, is docile, because docile pupils are going to attend classes regularly, pay the tuition on schedule, breed more pupils, and not cause any trouble. The sad thing about this is that docile beings, learning by rote, are not going to graduate from the fifth plane.

"So it is up to each driver to use the school and not let it use him. Take to heart all the manual has to offer on the HARMONY part. But rely on some very fine advice from the manual itself about the RIGHT PATH. 'The keys to the kingdom of heaven are within', and within means just what it says—within the vehicle, the navigator. When the driver restores communication with the navigator, he will find it easy to get back on the RIGHT PATH."

The oldtimer leaned forward, his voice serious and his finger stabbing at his listeners, "The revised manual, extolling the humble and the meek, is a tool for the teachers to gain control over the drivers. The original intent was to make the driver master his own huge ego in order for him to be able to hear the navigator—the still, small voice, the Godhood within."

A listener interrupted the oldtimer. "Could you straighten us on something? I'm not a racing fan, and some of your racing jargon is hard to follow, but I think I know what driving in HARMONY means—it's just living in harmony, isn't it? But I can't figure out the so-called "scoop" on the RIGHT PATH. What is it?"

The oldtimer grinned and nodded his head, making his halo bob. "You are right about the HARMONY bit. About the best I can say on the RIGHT PATH is to grow spiritually. All beings of whatever plane are there to experience and interact with other beings, and thru this experience, to learn to discern between actions which are beneficial to all concerned and actions that are detrimental, and then make the beneficial actions part of their being."

The questioner persisted. "The HEAD UMPIRE must be GOD, but who is he?"

The oldtimer threw back his head and laughed, a belly laugh that made the halo whip violently. "You sure can ask the simple questions. Well, I'm just a 5th plane type myself, and rumor has it that there could be as many as 89 planes, so your dart board is as good as mine, but here goes. I believe each being carries within itself a Divine Essence, our navigator, sent out from GOD. I think the sum total of all these Divine Essences, or centers of consciousness, is GOD. Now, those up around the 89th plane make the big decisions, but even we fifth plane types help mold our own future. Down there on that 'free-wheeling' planet, I think the thoughts and actions of all the drivers have a direct affect on the course of events there."

The oldtimer looked at his Timex and stood up. "I must relieve Pete at the gate now, but here is one last word. Try to get to know your navigator, your god within. You will find that he is, as one primitive society described him, the utterly trustworthy one. Remember, however, that the only way you can communicate with him is thru your CB operator. You must learn to shut out the conscious physical world and contact that little rascal, who in turn can put you in contact with the wisdom of your navigator. Then, thru your own experiences, shared and augmented by your CB operator and navigator, you can advance spiritually. But remember, the HEAD UMPIRE is looking for mature, seasoned, decision-making drivers, who are able to work with their CB operator and navigator like a fine-tuned engine. If we get cracking, maybe we will get the checkered flag in a few more heats, and not have to crawl back into those confounded gadgets ever again,—except when we want to."

As the oldtimer left, one of the listeners said to a friend, "Do you think what he said is for real?"

His friend shrugged, "Do you have any better ideas?"

The above glimpse of life in vehicles has hopefully flexed (blown?) the reader's mind enough so that we all can speculate intelligently on the scope of the "whole shebang". Back in the 1930s, Hubble and some other scientists developed the theory of an expanding universe. By checking the red shift in the light spectrum coming from a distant star, it seemed to indicate the stars are receding and the entire Universe is expanding. About 20 years later, Bondi, Gold, and Hoyle separately developed the idea of continuous creation, in which some areas of the Universe could be growing while other areas could be contracting. Mark's reading seems to confirm that this is so—if you have an overview of the whole shebang, some portions would be expanding and others contracting. We evidently see a very small slice of the Universe from our vantage point here on Earth.

Several esoteric sources have mentioned that the speed of light might not be the insurmountable barrier as calculated by Einstein. When Mark was asked in a reading about two decades ago, if the UFO which picked up Betty and Barney Hill and thoroughly examined them, was from a planet within range of our radio telescopes, the answer was no. Yes, the Universe is a large place. But just how large? Mark was asked if the Universe was really infinite. The answer given was that for our understanding, we could consider it infinite. The questioner persisted, asking how large was the Universe compared with the area of the Solar System. The answer was 10 to the 836th power.

Now the readings themselves have stated that figures in readings, where not aiding in spiritual growth, can be in error. We know nothing about the area of the Solar System or how 10 to the 836th power would equate. We are just throwing the figures out on the table, also with the inkling that the Universe may not be infinite.

One more word about infinity. When asked in a reading with Mark about how many planes of existence there were (humans on Earth are reputed to be in the fifth plane), the answer was 89, "at which level beings approach infinity". No; we don't know what that means either.

It is hoped that some of the unconventional wisdom in this chapter will aid in the expressed goal of this book—making the reader start thinking about things rarely considered before.

WHERE DID WE COME FROM?

In the prologue, it was promised that three important questions would be addressed, which are what the author calls the three Ws. What could be more important than finding out *Where* we come from, *Why* we are here, and *Where* do we go from here?

First things first—where and how did the human race originate? There are several theories. One 17th century Irish Bishop, James Ussher, by counting the begats in the Old Testament, calculated that Adam had been created by God in the year 4004 B.C. That figure was accepted by many well into the 20th century.

The next theory, proposed by Charles Darwin in the 19th century, claimed that humans had evolved from the same primate branch of mammals as the apes, who had evolved from other extinct animals, who had evolved from fish, who had evolved from single cell creatures. Each of these changes had taken ages to accomplish.

The churches fought Darwin's theory, but new finds in Anthropology and Geology appear to bear him out. So today the majority of the scientific community has convinced the majority of the nonscientific community that humans did, indeed, evolve from the same tree as the apes.

The evolution of humans has been pretty well accepted by all and we have gone on to questions like how did the first spark of life on Earth originate? Could it be a bolt of lightning energizing some amino acid cells? Or could it be transpermia; the movement of spores thru space. Weighty problems, indeed.

But back to humans. Some 3 or 4 millions years ago, Australopithecus, a toolmaker and social animal appeared who just may have been one of our predecessors, or at least from a common branch. This little rascal is described by anthropologists as a toolmaker, but as Robert Aubrey points out in his book, *African Genesis*, he was really more of a weapons maker. His cave homes reveal a multitude of skeletal remains of all kinds of animals with one thing in common—an indentation in the skull into which the large joint of an antelope's humerus bone fitted perfectly. This little 90 pound wonder had discovered that by breaking off the small end of the limb, he had created the perfect club. Each one of his caves had an abundance of these weapons.

If he was our ancestor, we have come by our seeming love of weapons naturally. He was the toughest kid, for his size, on the block—all kinds of larger and stronger animals could be found in the bone yard of this little carnivore. Yes, the more we think about it, the more we can see him as an ancestor of the human race.

Less than two millions years ago, a fairly large-brained ape-like animal, Homo Erectus, appeared in Africa and spread to Europe and Asia. He had dexterous hands, walked upright, controlled fire, probably had some language skills, and was also a good "tool-maker". And our own Homo Sapiens arrived recently, though by most to be at least 35,000 years ago.

So, we have one theory of God creating humans; and another of them evolving from apes. Do we have any other ideas? One might question that if we are not created by God, or evolved from lower animals on Earth, what is left?

Well, there are a few other possibilities, one of which we will explore. When one first picks up Zacharia Sitchin's *The Twelfth Planet*, the first thought is that it is a great sci-fi adventure. But like both Velikovsky and Cayce, the more one reads, the more sense Sitchin makes. Let us grasp the lance firmly, while we tilt with yet another windmill.

Sitchin postulates that people from another planet, the Nefilim of the Bible, landed on Earth and established outposts for the sole purpose of gathering materials, particularly rare metals, to be sent back to their home planet. The Sumerian texts state that their main interplanetary base was in Sumer, in ancient Mesopotania, with the mining operation in Africa.

Their planet was in reality a comet that Sitchin figures orbited around the Sun once every 3600 years. Now, this puts quite a strain on our imagination—here are some beings digging ore out of the ground in Africa year after year which must be refined, shipped to Sumer, loaded onto a spaceship, and sent to their home planet, a planet which orbited close to our Sun only once in every 3600 years! Come on, now! You've got to be kidding! Well, Sitchin had the answer; these people had the secret of eternal life and lived incredibly long lifetimes.

It doesn't take a mind reader to guess what the reader is thinking. If you were gods with the secret of eternal life and all kinds of smarts, would you spend centuries mining ore in a hot, humid hole in Africa—no siree!

Well, believe it or not, that is just what the Nefilim working in the mines thought, too. In fact, maybe we humans are here today because the miners, the working class of the Nefilim called the Anunnaki, went on strike! They surrounded the guest house of the area boss, Enlil, there on an inspection tour, and demanded that a primitive worker be created to ease their hardship. The Sumerian Records state their need vividly;

> "Let a lulu, a primitive worker, be created,
>   While the birth goddess is present,
>   Let her create a primitive worker.
>   Let him bear the yoke—
>   Let him carry the toil of the gods."

Now, this took a lot more genetic engineering than we know about today, but even the Nefilim had a lot of trial and error attempts. The ancients recorded some of their false starts; half horse, half Nefilim and half bull, half Nefilim were attempts to find an assistant for the Anunnaki. But finally they hit on the right combination. As Sitchin describes in his book, "The animal was available, but Homo Erectus posed a problem. On the one hand, he was too intelligent and wild to become simply a docile beast of burden. On the other hand, he was not really suited to the task. His physique had to be changed. He had to be able to grasp and use the tools of the Anunnaki, walk and bend like them, so he could replace the gods in the fields and the mines. He had to have a better brain—not like those of the Anunnaki, but enough to understand speech and commands and the tasks allotted to him. He needed enough cleverness and understanding to be an obedient and useful "Amelu"—a serf!

One word here about the term Nefilim. Sitchin explained that as a youth, he studied Genesis in the original Hebrew. When the teacher taught about the time when God resolved to destroy Mankind with the Great Flood, the sons of the deities, who took the daughters of Man, were upon the Earth. The Hebrew original called these deities Nefilim; the teacher explained that it meant giants, but Sitchin objected; didn't it mean literally "those who were cast down", who had descended to Earth? He was reprimanded and told to accept the current interpretation. This started Sitchin on his quest for the truth.

Getting back to the genetic engineering, they decided to make an Adapa, a primitive man, as the Sumerian records call him, in the image (selem) and likeness (Dmut) of the Nefilim. He lacked only the divine span of life, high intelligence, and certain "knowing."

The texts indicate that the ovum of a female Homo Erectus, fertilized by a male Nefilim, was genetically altered and then placed in the womb of a high princess for the normal process of pregnancy and birth. Adapa, the primitive worker, was created!

And his mate, too, but not from a rib. The Sumerian word TI has two meanings; one is rib, and the other is essence, or life essence. After they had agreed that the male Adapa was an acceptable serf, they created a female counterpart from the male's life essence. And then they started making many of them by using the implants in birth goddesses.

At this point, the Adapas could not reproduce. Remember that hybrids, such as mules, cannot reproduce. This may have been by design—the Nefilim wanted to keep track of how many serfs they had created. Sitchin found nothing in the texts about the serpent and the apple in the garden of Eden. His guess is that the area boss, Enlil, did not want them to reproduce. Enlil was a harsh boss. He had wanted to execute the Anunnaki when they went out on a strike. The immediate boss, Enki, had backed the Anunnaki's demand for a worker to be created. During a big meeting on the subject, presided over by the chief boss, Ani, the majority of the Nefilim had sided with Enki, and the go-ahead for the Adapa's (Man) creation was given.

The first batch of Adapas was sent to Enki, in Africa, to provide the muscle to help the Anunnaki mine ore. But Enlil demanded and got a batch to grow food for the Anunnaki working at the space station in Sumer. This was the Garden of Eden. The total number of colonists on Earth was not large. Sitchin speculates that the total number of Nefilim on Earth was only about 300. They were merely a mining outpost.

Sitchin theorizes that Enki was the serpent of the Bible. Enki had been the force behind the creation of Man, after the strike of the Anunnaki. Indeed, the first fertilized ovum for the Adapa had been placed in the womb of his mate, Ninki. Enki and Enlil had never gotten along together. Time and time again, Enki had showed compassion for his hard-working Anunnaki and later for his Adapas. He wanted to make the Adapas able to reproduce, but did not dare to further alter genetically one of his mining serfs in Africa because Enlil would know that Enki had a hand in it. Instead, it is possible that Enki, on one of his few visits to Sumer, slipped into the pea patch (the Garden of Eden) and secretly altered one of the female Adapas there, enabling her to conceive. This was truly the first Eve.

The question of whether a male Adapa had to be altered too, is up for grabs; the author thinks that it was done, else there might have been a lot of fruitless time wasted when male and female Adapas worked together.

But the question can be raised as to why female workers were produced at all. The author, not Sitchin, has a theory; those Anunnaki working in the mines and the fields needed male Adapas to do the hard work for them, but they also needed relaxation and sexual release. As there were probably few Nefilim female among the spartan mining colony, what better companion would there be to have than a sterile female who looked just like themselves and obeyed orders. Whether she derived any pleasure was a moot point—she was a serf and did what she was told.

Soon, however, Enlil found out about the creative abilities of Adam and Eve, either by the clothing as indicated in the Bible, or more likely, the signs of Eve's pregnancy. Enlil immediately threw both of them out of the pea patch, and for good reason—he didn't want the Anunnaki consorting with those new, sexually aroused female Adapas, who would produce a mixed race with inferior genes and characteristics.

So Adam and Eve and their offspring had to roam in the Zacros mountains outside of the pea patch. After many generations, they were invited back to Sumer, but the reason for this change of heart is not given. Eventually, the same old problem arose; the Nefilim males evidently liked the responding fertile female Adapas better than the lifeless sterile ones, and many inferior mixed offspring resulted. If your life span as a Nefilim was tens of thousands of years, as suggested by Sitchin, you would be unhappy with a flood of children who would live only 900 years.

The Sumerian Texts (written by Adapas, remember) blamed the hardships endured by the Adapas (Man), such as floods and famines, on the Nefilim. This was done by the Nefilim *not* telling Man in advance of upcoming natural devastation. But to no avail—Man just kept on increasing and spread around the globe.

Finally, the Nefilim bosses became aware of an upcoming gigantic world-wide flood. Sitchin postulates that it was caused by the Antarctic Ice Cap suddenly breaking away, causing a mammoth tidal wave and raising of the ocean level (this seems improbably, although it is difficult to figure out what would raise the water levels world-wide for months on end if it wasn't the Arctic Ice Cap). Whatever the cause, the Nefilim must have known the time of this natural onslaught to the hour (which is why the cause doesn't sound like the Antarctic Ice Cap—it's breakup would have been too unpredictable).

Enlil wanted to make certain that no one alerted Man to this danger, so that none of them would survive. He did not trust Enki at all, so he made Enki swear before the whole council that he, Enki, would not warn any of Mankind. In this Sumerian version of Noah and the Ark, written before 3800 B.C., Enki got around his vow by placing a leader of Mankind behind a reed screen and then thinking out loud abut the approaching great flood. When the man behind the screen was told by Enki to build a boat, he replied that he didn't know how to build a boat. If the readers had heard Bill Cosby's skit on Noah, they would appreciate the resulting dialog; Enki tells the human, in detail, how to build the Sumerian Ark.

In the Sumerian texts, their "Noah" was to batten down the hatches of the "sulili" (also the current Hebrew word for submarine) when the head of the space port at Sippar ordered "a trembling at dusk and caused a shower down, a rain of eruptions." This meant that when all the Nefilim boarded their spacecraft at Sippar and blasted off, it was time to brace for the wall of water.

After the Flood occurred, the sulili floated for 5 months before it finally grounded on a mountain top and it was 11 months before they could leave the ship and live on dry land, identical to the Biblical version. They also sent out birds, as did the Bible. When they were first able to get out on solid ground, they sacrificed an animal in thanksgiving and were roasting it—when the spaceships of the Nefilim landed beside them.

Enlil was mad to find the earthlings still alive but only for a moment. Things had changed—it sounds as though the space ships had not been provisioned for such a long orbital period because the Nefilim were starving and frightened when they landed. They *needed* Man and his labor! But was this the only reason for their change of heart towards Man?

This first meeting after the Flood, and the change in direction of the policies of the Nefilim, must be reviewed and debated. Before the Flood, according to Sitchin, there were few domesticated animals and no domesticated grains. The Nefilim had only small bases, were few in number, and probably kept their pea patches under close guard, as they must have had domesticated grains imported from their home planet.

But after the Flood, everything changed. Domesticated grains, which agronomists insist would take centuries of high tech effort to develop, appeared in profusion. New types of domesticated animals appeared everywhere. And the Nefilim developed a plan to reconstruct the devastated Earth in four major areas. The first was, of course, Sumer, and the spaceports were rebuilt brick by brick on the same sites. The second was Egypt, the third was the Indus Valley in India, and the fourth was the "Holy Place". The original meaning of the term holy, according to Sitchin, was dedicated and restricted. The Nefilim named this place Tilmon, which means literally, "the place of the missiles". Where was this place? Sitchin ended his book with this question.

Let us look back to the pre-Deluge days and review the roles of the three Nefilim bosses. Enki, the engineer of the group, ran the mining operation in Africa. Enlil handled the spaceport operation in Sumer and trade in the Mediterranean. Ani ruled the "heavenly abode", which could have been the home planet itself, or a space station in orbit around the Earth. The space station idea sounds the more feasible to the author.

The author thinks that what accounted for the happiness of the Nefilim on finding that Man had survived the Flood, was the possibility of devastation on the home planet of the Nefilim.

According to Sitchin's interpretation of the texts, their planet Marduk orbited around the Sun once very 3600 years, and it was passing thru the Solar System at the time of the Flood (it *caused* the Flood!). The author, not Sitchin, suggests that in this close pass by the Earth, a great cataclysm took place on Marduk, as well as the Earth.

The description, in the Sumerian texts, of the cataclysm on Earth as seen from the spaceships is vivid. The Mother Goddess, who created the first Adapa, bewailed what she was seeing. She wept and spoke of seeing her creatures die. They filled the rivers like dragonflies, their fatherhood taken by the rolling sea.

Suppose, after the Nefilim gazed down on the vast destruction on Earth, they fearfully took the short hop to their own planet, which had just completed it's rampage thru the Solar System, and found it in the same condition as the Earth; completely devastated. Suppose, all of a sudden, the highest high tech items in the Solar system were a few space ships and possibly a space station in orbit around the Earth. No more high tech planet to supply them with high tech replacements. It would mean they would have to start to rebuild their space capability almost from scratch.

The first thing the Nefilim did, after the Flood, was to make a pact with Man. They needed him! They wouldn't let floods or famine strike Man again without warning him. In return, Man was to multiply and provide labor for the Nefilim. Translators have stated that Man was to worship God, but in the original Sumerian Texts, it clearly states that Man was to *WORK* for, not worship, the gods we call the Nefilim (the Old Testament in most instances, but not all, changed the term Gods to the monotheistic God).

A question immediately comes to mind; why didn't the Nefilim start manufacturing the sterile Adapas again? One reason might be that no Homo Erectus survived the Flood.

Let us look, for a moment, at the calendar Sitchin developed for the Nefilim's sojourn on Earth. By looking at the Sumerian texts for the years of rule of the Nefilim leaders, Sitchin figured they must have first arrived about 445,000 B.C. He did this by cross checking the ages the rulers lived in with the zodiac signs and the stars involved and their locations at the time. He puts the mutiny of the Anunnaki and the creation of Man at about

300,000 B.C., and the Flood at about 13,000 B.C.

For thousands of years before the Flood, the Nefilim had Man available to do all of the physical labor, the mining and the farming and building. The Anunnaki, the past laborers among the Nefilim, were now the supervisors of Man. After the Flood, in the three areas they rebuilt, they set up the structure of Kingship to rule. They would appoint a person to rule the country and carry out the orders of the Nefilim. For many centuries, in Egypt and the Middle East, the countries involved had a tradition of a person assuming the throne of a country "with the advice and consent of the gods". It appears that the Nefilim withdrew to the fourth area, the Holy Place, in order to both separate themselves from Man and to concentrate on finding a new home planet from themselves. It appears they didn't want to remain on this old catastrophic Earth, and it was probable that their old planet, Marduk, was now even a less desirable home than Earth. We note that the mining area of Africa was not one of the places mentioned to be rebuilt, possibly intimating that no more rare metals were needed for a now lifeless home planet.

The Nefilim ruled the growing numbers of Man, multiplying after the Flood, with rulers they appointed and instructed how to accomplish various tasks. These rulers were given all kinds of assistance by the Nefilim; not only domesticated grains and animals, but building designs, math systems, metal refining techniques, and laws. The Nefilim themselves, it appears to the author, moved to the Holy Area. The leaders they chose to rule the developing countries may well have been some of the offspring of "the sons of the gods who mated with the daughters of man" we read about in the Bible. The life span of these half Nefilim, half human offspring may have been the 900 years also mentioned in the Bible.

It appears that as the centuries rolled by, the role of the Nefilim as leaders, thru the use of kingship, lessened and finally vanished. For almost two millennia now, the statement made during the coronation of rulers, "by and with the consent of God (and earlier 'the gods')", which at one time was the most important part of the whole ritual, has become simply a flowery phrase.

Imagine, if you will, in ancient Egypt after a cataclysm, no emissary arriving from the Nefilim with instructions and, more importantly, no replacements for the aging ruler and his wife, both of whom are half Nefilim and half human. They finally die, leaving a son and a daughter. The son, now the ruler, must wed so as to continue the line, since no further word has been heard from the Nefilim. If he marries a human, any offspring might lose part or all of his semi-divine life span of 900 years. Or should he marry his sister, thus assuring that his offspring would retain the life span, but risking the problems of inbreeding. From the ancient records of Egypt, it appears that several Pharaohs were faced with this problem, and chose the latter route.

Now back to the problem; where was the Holy Area? One possibility is the continent of Atlantis, rumored by Plato to be in the Atlantic Ocean. With that idea, another possibility emerges; what if there was no space station or heavenly abode", but Ani had been over in Atlantis all the time. When the Nefilim had told Man they were flying out into space to the heavenly abode, it might have been a trick to keep Man from knowing they were simply flying to another part of the Earth.

Getting tired of problems? One more little one. If the Nefilim's planet, Marduk, was indeed in a 3600 year orbit around the Sun, it would be quite a hop for a spaceship leaving the Earth when Marduk was at its greatest distance from the Solar System. The space ship would have to approach or exceed the speed of light in order to make the trip in a realistic time period.

Now for a look at an interesting factor about this remote mining colony on Earth in ancient times. Did the Nefilim on Earth live a life typical of the life the average Nefilim led back on the home planet?

If we look at some mother country-colony relationships here on Earth, we can find great differences. The life of the Spanish Conquistadors in the New World versus their home life in Spain was almost a Jeykell and Hyde disparity. A look at the Athens in Pericles time is also intriguing. Amazed by the output of all things during the Golden Age of Democracy in Greece, we asked at the museum in Athens what was the role of the free citizen in the Athens of Pericles. We knew there were some slaves which we assumed were the backbone of the labor on the Acropolis and other public projects. But what about the free citizens in this great democracy?

gist of the answers we got was enlightening. If you, as a
man, were going any enterprise acceptable to your fellow
zens which put food on your table and a roof over your head,
at was fine. If you were unable to put food on your table and a
roof over your head, you could go on their version of
welfare—you could (1) work on the Acropolis or other public
projects or (2) voluntarily leave to work in one of the many
Athenian trading ports around the Mediterranean. Either choice
would guarantee minimum food on the table and a roof over
your own and fellow workers' heads.

It is the author's opinion, not Sitchin's, that on Marduk, to
go on an expedition to set up and endlessly operate a mining
colony on a distant planet known to experience periodic
cataclysms was definitely the pits! On far off Marduk, would you
have *volunteered* to go to such a place and dig ore out of the
ground for centuries? The sound of it has all the trappings of a
penal colony. It makes one think of the settlement of Australia
using prisoners.

What if—here goes some crystal ball work by the author
again! What if the typical Anunnaki, the working stiff of the
Nefilim, was at worst a prisoner, like the pressed seamen of the
British Navy during the 18th century, or at the best the lowest
level of society on the home planet? It would also appear that the
fearless leaders of this motley crew would not be of the highest
caliber. If there were any signs of a rotation system of command
between the colony and the home planet, this would not be an
obvious conclusion. But the bosses reigns were spelled out from
the first landing. And the moral life of some of these leaders
makes Payton Place sound tame.

(As a sort of a seventh inning stretch, let us take a long look
at the two halves of Man's possible progenitors. In one corner,
we have Homo Erectus, an excellent weapons maker and behind
him in the misty past we have that lethal little 90 pounder,
Australopithecus, with his club. In the other corner, we have
either the dregs of society or the felons of a more advanced
world. Combine those two lines and what kind of a vehicle do
you get. Humans! No wonder we humans are such a cantankerous
bunch! But maybe it is the ideal brain and vehicle combination to
work out our kind of problems.)

By now, some of the readers out there must be twisting

uncomfortably in their seats. They are *certain* that except for a very, very remote possibility of eons spent shoveling coal into a furnace, they will most likely spend eternity sitting on white clouds, strumming harps, and having good conversations with other wing-equipped beings, after living their three score and ten years on Earth.

They also feel if by some ridiculous fluke, they did have to come back and live other lifetimes on the Earth before evolving on to the next plane, that next plane surely must be sweetness and light, "manned" by good godlike beings, who never err, sin, swear, or run down their peers As the old saying goes, it aint necessarily so.

From several sources, we have been told that human beings here on Earth are vehicles for souls in the fifth plane of evolution, and that this plane is a wild one—one in which the soul has the most free will and the least control of just about any plane. Some say that this level is really one hell of a place.

Boy, when we get to that sixth plane, we must really turn over a new leaf, or do we? When we graduated from the 5th grade to the 6th grade in elementary school, did we become a totally different person? Not really!

Because there are so many planes to evolve thru, here on this fifth plane we can hardly conceive of perfection. Instead of talking about the straight and narrow path that many preach about, we are fortunate if we happen to stumble in the right *direction*. But our main reason for being on this Earth is to stumble, of our own volition, in that right direction. For our Godhood knows not only the right direction, but also the straight and narrow path, and can only nod when we, the conscious mind, stumble in the right direction due to a stimulus deep within us. This action is much better than moving due to a majority social, political, or religious flow, and this action surely makes our Godhood smile.

How did we get into this?—back to the Nefilim. The last little detour was a means of stating that even if the colony of Nefilims on Earth were sixth plane beings, they might not be covered with angel dust (oops! sorry; wrong term) Who knows; they might be only fifth plane beings. But did you ever think about Man—did he get to be a fifth plane type by being half way between a sixth plane Nefilim and a fourth plane Homo Erectus?

It's only a thought—it adds up, though, mathematically speaking.

The author has been asked whether he thinks Sitchin is correct? Well, in reading the book, *The Twelfth Planet*, it is difficult to believe that the Nefilim evolved on this Earth. One of the most amazing texts tells of their method of entering the Solar System from outer space. The texts depict rocket ships with detachable modules on the front. Remember that these texts were written at least 5800 years ago, and the planet Pluto in our Solar System was not discovered by modern man until 1930. The texts state that after passing the three smaller, outer planets (Pluto, Neptune, and Uranus), they gaze at the great size of the fourth and fifth planets (Saturn and Jupiter), and of having to put on their MEs, or pressure suits, while passing thru the asteroid belt between Jupiter and Mars. And finally, they prepare for a landing on Earth, which is No. 7. Counting from outer space, Earth is NO. 7. To us heliocentric oriented types living on Earth, we are No. 3, out from the Sun.

The story of the Nefilim's creation of Man does sound a bit wild, but it seems as plausible as any other theory around. Because the creation of only one of the five races of Man was covered does not mean that other efforts were not going on in other places.

There is a question from out there—are the theories of Sitchin and Velikovsky compatible? It appears that for the most part they are. Velikovsky described the last three cataclysms to rack planet Earth as being in the 15th and 8th centuries B.C., while Sitchin's Flood must have been before the Sumerian Civilization, carbon dated at 3800 B.C. They were events in different time periods.

The only discrepancy between the two about which the author feels uncomfortable is their treatment of the planet Venus. Sitchin claims it was in its proper place in the Solar System as long ago as 445,000, whereas Velikovsky states that it was a newcomer, a comet torn from the side of Jupiter fairly recently (still hot from the birth), in a long period orbit around the Sun, periodically coming in from outer space and causing all kinds of ruckuses.

Either one or the other author is incorrect, or the possibility exists that Venus was in its regular orbit prior to the Sumerian Texts but was forced into an irregular orbit later. Then, with the last pass in the 8th century B.C., it returned to a position similar to its original orbit. NO! NO! It is a million to one chance it would return to its old position and it would mean too early a date for its birth from Jupiter. Problems! Problems! The author sides with Velikovsky on this one, as so many of his assumptions about Venus have proven to be true.

So where are we? It appears that the Earth was colonized by non-earthlings in the past. The date of the first attempt could be long before the appearance of the Nefilim. One of Mark's readings places the first try (unsuccessful) at 30 million years ago.

One version of the first colonists on Earth was given by George Adamski in his book, *Inside The Spaceships*. He was told by beings from space, who gave him a joy ride out to the moon and back, that colonists from their planet had long ago established a colony on Earth, but discovered later that the Earth periodically had cataclysms caused by, they thought, the planet having only one moon. Because of this fact they abandoned their colony, taking most of the beings back to the home planet. Because of the apparent beauty of this planet at the time, a few colonists chose to remain, in spite of no high tech and the probability of cataclysms. These beings, Adamski thought, might be the origin of some of the early ape men. Thru a process of devolution, these beings might have survived floods, famines, and fires, not to speak of saber-toothed tigers, but at a great cost, both physically and mentally. The author is of the opinion that devolution of that nature can occur as readily as evolution. The survivors of a great ancient civilization, smashed by a massive cataclysm, may become little better than the animals they hunted or were hunted by. Incidentally, Mark's reading confirmed that Adamski did, indeed, go for a ride in the spaceship.

Sitchin has a shrew explanation for the similarity of the Homo Erectus and the Nefilim, physique-wise. If the Earth did periodically pass thru the tail of the comet (whether Venus, Marduk, or some other long period comet), it is quite possible that the DNA of many of its animals fell to the Earth. This idea of worlds "seeding" each other in close passage is gaining many advocates.

One might ask if the human form is a common form

throughout the Universe. Not knowing the intent of the Divine Mind, one can only speculate. The fact that almost all of the UFO reports on beings observed indicate they are bipeds with two arms and a head, ranging from those four feet tall, green and with no ears and huge eyes, thru very human-appearing beings, to the eight foot tall hairy Sasquatches. This indicates one of two things; either the observers don't have the imagination to dream up a real good monster for their fake, attention-getting tale (which some of them are), or biped humanoid shapes are fairly common, at least in this neck of the woods. This would give credence to the idea of a Divine Mind being behind the whole shebang; left to evolution, and no seeding of DNA, the most intelligent being in the Universe just might have 12 legs and 12 arms, or even be a green slime.

The author believes, however, that we as evolve into higher planes, a physical body becomes of lesser importance, and also that intelligent life can come in many forms. More of this in a later chapter.

Many people think if the Earth was colonized in the past, any UFO contacts now would be part of a well-coordinated master plan, with each ship in touch with all the others. It need not be that way; contacts can be simply chance landings from diverse sources. It is analogous to a South Sea island being discovered first by a British sailing ship, and then visited in turn by random Dutch, American, and French ships.

Mark's reading concerning the motive for the reputed temporary abduction of Betty and Barney Hill in 1966, by beings from a spaceship, is fascinating. Although the Hills could only remember seeing the spaceship from a distance, under hypnotic regression by a doctor (not Mark), they described in detail being immobilized and carried aboard the spaceship, where they were given a through physical exam. Mark's reading said the interest of the space beings in the Hills was "that of a small boy examining a captured butterfly".

Now for the big question. What became of the Nefilim? Sitchin speculates that the Nefilim's creation, Man, gradually crowded its creators off the Earth. How could this happen? How could this serf crowd his masters off the Earth, armed as they were with "awesome weapons and spaceships"?

Let us construct a hypothesis. Suppose the Flood *did* wipe

out all high tech on Marduk and at the most all the Nefilim had were their spaceships, circling the Earth with the evacuees gazing down on the devastation, plus a space station, miraculously still in orbit. At the least, they had just the spaceships (which condition is hard to say—a cataclysm that would cause the Flood would probably destroy the space station).

If Marduk was devastated as well, where did all the domesticated grains and animals come from to restock the Earth after the Flood? The best possibility would be *another* surviving colony of the Nefilim. When one thinks about it it would seem strange if the only Nefilim outpost would be a 300 being mining effort on Earth. Looking around the Mediterranean in ancient times, we see city states and nations with many trading outposts. Why not Marduk?

When this approach is taken, one problem looms immediately. Where could any planets be located within the range of Nefilim spaceships that would be suitable for colonies? Currently, it is thought that only our Earth's environment could support Man in our Solar System. But was this true prior to the 8th century B.C. battle in the sky between the Earth, Mars, and Venus? Before this time, Mars and/or Venus might have sustained the Nefilim. But even if no such other planet in the Solar System, the readings state that space ships able to exceed the speed of light were once based on Atlantis, making other Nefilim colonies in other systems quite possible.

Back to the problem; how did the Nefilim, with their weapons and spaceships, lose out to Man? If Marduk was devastated by its encounter with the Earth during the time of the Flood, the Nefilim's space capability may have been crippled as well. Imagine a United States space station orbiting the Earth, in dire need of a GM65438A fuel pump, but the U.S.A. had been obliterated in a nuclear war.

So, with the Flood behind them, the Nefilim made peace with Man, and with Man doing the work, rebuilt four major areas of the Earth. This industrial base was needed to aid them in their single-minded struggle—to regain interstellar transportation. When they reached their goal, they searched the Universe for a more perfect world than this chaotic Earth and on finding it, moved most of their people to it. They left a few rulers in Atlantis to govern it and provide Kingship to other countries on Earth.

After some time, our tempermental Earth started acting up again. Atlantis started to submerge, over long periods of time, into the Atlantic Ocean. This was too much for the Nefilim; they evacuated their rulers from Atlantis, leaving the rest of the people to fend for themselves. They had experienced enough of this fickle world, and those dumb, short-lived, but durable serfs they had spawned. They may have tried to enforce Kingship from afar, after the evacuation, but may well have finally, within the last two millennia, just washed their hands of Earth; good riddance!

By this time, the majority of the people on Atlantis were quite a mixture. Plato describes every race from black to white as inhabitants of Atlantis. This is probably the site of the other attempts to create an Adapa, many centuries earlier. At any rate, they fled in all directions as the land continued to submerge.

A good book on Atlantis, *Atlantis, the Antediluvian World*, was written by Ignacious Donnelly in the 1890s. He depicts a typical village of the Mandan Indians in North Dakota. Many of the tribe were light-skinned, with hazel, gray, or blue eyes. Their villages were built in a circle around a 150 foot meeting ground, in the center of which was located a 8 to 10 foot diameter hogshead, crudely made of hoops and planks, which was called the "Big Canoe".

Annually, a play was performed—an Indian, his body smeared with white ashes, would approach the village and go around to each hut. He said he was Nu-mohk-muck-a-non (the one and only man) and he was the only survivor of "a sad catastrophe on Earth which happened with the overflowing of the waters". He said he came in a big canoe from across the waters to the east. He had come now to collect a tool from each household to put in the Big Canoe for its maintenance. At the end of the annual ritual, the tools were thrown into the deepest part of the river as a means of appeasing the gods, so they wouldn't cause an overflowing of the waters to reoccur.

Donnelly thinks this tradition was handed down thru centuries on Atlantis and later during the tribal wanderings. Plato, in the *Timaeus*, tells of the destruction of Atlantis, due to a series of subsidations. Can you imagine the fear in a village in Atlantis that had survived one subsidation by climbing into a huge hogshead, building a new village while maintaining the hogshead for yet another submerging. They *Knew*, from experience, because that contraption had saved their lives.

And at last, the final submergence, and one survivor being washed ashore on North America. He found a new mate, and started a new tribe. We don't have to wonder why he insisted on the maintenance of the Big Canoe. His insistence was so persuasive that untold centuries later, his descendants still built their huts around a replica of the Big Canoe and ritually contributed to its maintenance.

Part of this annual event was a dance performed by 12 men. Two were painted black, two vermilion, and several white. As Plato related, Atlanteans came in all colors.

The old Inca texts show that a red-bearded white race who, long ago, arrived in Peru from the northeast. After living there for some time, they built reed rafts and sailed westward into the sunset, rather than fight a war-like Indian tribe that moved in on them. Atlanteans? Nefilim offshoots?

Wait a minute. There is a question out there. Do we have any other ideas of where and how the human race originated? Jumpin' Johosaphet! You people out there are missing the whole point! The main idea of this chapter is to get that thing, sitting on your shoulders and keeping your ears apart, to be something more than just a hat rack. How do *YOU* think the human race originated! This chapter is simply the result of grabbing a book from the library shelf and doing some mental exercises. Why don't you do the same. Or better yet, *YOU* read Sitchin, Cayce, and Velikovsky and books you will discover on your own, and develop your own theories. Once again, this is the purpose of this book—to tickle your imagination and to get creative thoughts flowing.

Mark was asked in a reading about the validity of Sitchin and said the following, "This is thru the dark veil. It appears as an allegory. It is a corruption of the original records. It contains an element of truth."

"Did space people create Man?"

"That's an oversimplification of a complicated process. You can say they had a hand in it—we are looking at something that took a very long time. It did not originate here and went thru a number of phases and stages at a number of places. The adaptation of the bodies inhabited by Man—this was a process of bringing together a number of good works from a number of places and the five races were the efforts of five different givers of life. And not so much a competition to find the winner but an effort that happened to be simultaneous, with essentially five results."

"How can the author separate facts from fiction?"

"I don't see how. He would have to be intuitive,. He would have to apply his own intuition to it."

The reader must know the author well enough by now to know that he has an opinion on just about every subject. Well, intuition was exercised and, rightly or wrongly, it is felt that Sitchin's overall interpretation of the texts is stumbling in the right direction. If the author was a few years younger, he would like to jump in a take a look at those Sumerian Texts, but he does think visitors from another world created Man. The Deities may have been the generating force, but beings did the nut and bolts construction work. The Sumerian Texts may be an oversimplification of what really happened, as viewed by the descendants of one of the five races of serfs created about the same time. When you consider the serfs were barred from the space ports and medical laboratories, it is amazing they were able to interpret as well as they did just what went on in the "forbidden areas guarded by the gods with the awesome weapons."

It appears that the need for an Adapa was acted on throughout the Nefilim Empire and Sumer was just one giver or life, and the others were elsewhere on Earth or on some other world or worlds. It is similar to Ford, Chevrolet, Honda, Jeep, and VW coming out with different vehicles. The texts cover only one effort.

The reading stated that these texts seem to be a corruption of the original records. From studying the Bible, the author has seen how meanings can change, either accidentally or deliberately, when records are recopied and translated by various people for various reasons. But it is felt there is definitely an element of truth here.

It must be admitted this is the most garbled, incoherent, repetitious and, yes, intriguing chapter in the book. If these things did happen to the Nefilim and their creation, Man, trying to fill in the How and Why of things occurring is mind-boggling. Each time a new attempt is made to rewrite it, new ideas and solutions sprung forth like runners from a strawberry plant. The author is now to the point of not wanting to touch it for a while, just let it simmer. Maybe it will be tackled in some future book, probably entitled *Hindsight On Hindsight*.

Now, if you don't agree with some of the conclusions in the chapter, don't get mad, swear, and throw away the book; write your own book! That is what this chapter and book are all about. To get the mental juices flowing.

There are many cracks in the armor of conventional wisdom in many fields, waiting for your lance to find them. Pick up your lance, or in this case your quill (or pencil, typewriter, or computer) and join in the attempt to "stumble towards the truth." And Sitchin is a good takeoff spot. When one thinks of how the Nefilim may have shaped Man's history on Earth, it gives many rational explanations for Man's seemingly odd behavior at times in the distant past.

THE MIND

Tom Allen stirred in his sleep. A noise and an odor caused him to awake. Now he knew what it was; he heard the crackle of flames in the hall outside of his dormitory room and could smell the smoke coming in thru the open window. His mind, still groggy from sleep, spun round and round. What should he do?

He staggered to the window and looked out—no fire escape from his fourth floor window. He sobbed and looked nervously towards the door. At that very moment, the door itself started to burn. What should he do? Not enough time to tie sheets together, and the four story jump would kill me. What to do???

Tom ran around the room aimlessly, wringing his hands and screaming for help. Finally, he stood in the middle of the room, eyes rolling, saliva trickling down his chin, and his whole body sweating, both from the rising temperature and from fear.

Then a transformation took place. His eyes narrowed to slits. He took deep gulps of air into his lungs thru his open mouth. Reaching down to the foot of his bed, he snatched a heavy blanket and draped it over his head and upper body. Walking to the door, he kicked it down and ran into the hall. Glancing both ways from under the blanket, he ran to the right down the hallway, down the stairs, and finally out into the courtyard. Throwing off the burning blanket, Tom ran over to where a group of students were gathered. His roommate, Jerry, grabbed his arm and asked, "Are you all right, Tom? We thought everyone was already out!"

Tom blinked and finally focused his eyes on Jerry. "What happened? How did I get out here?"

Dianetics, by L. Ron Hubbard, explains just what happened to Tom, how his mind operated in that emergency, and also contains a most fascinating and plausible explanation of how the mind functions. Hubbard had an engineering background the likens the mind to a computer. This computer is normally operated by the reflective mind, which assimilates all the new data received by the senses prior to it being storied in the standard data banks.

As an example, a man *sees* a two year old Audi car being driven down the street, *hears* a miss in the engine, and *smells* the smokey exhaust. Each of these sensations are comprehended and assimilated by the reflective mind before being stored in the standard data banks. When a decision is needed on what kind of a car to buy, all kinds of data is pulled out of the banks—price comparisons, rides taken in different cars, and data on the durability of different makes and models. When the reflective mind considers durability, very likely it will call up the visual image of that Audi, and the sound of the miss in the engine, and the smell of the exhaust. These impressions, along with many others, will be used to make a decision on which car to buy.

This computer, according to Hubbard, functions perfectly. The reflective mind makes perfect use of the data in the standard data banks, arriving at the best possible decision every time. The reader may immediately ask why do so many people make such bad decisions?

Hubbard's answer is intriguing. He states that during times of either intense physical pain or painful emotion, the reflective mind is tuned out and that a primitive "reactive" mind takes over. When Tom's reflective mind threw in the sponge on how to get the body out of the burning room, the old primitive reactive mind came to the rescue.

As the sophisticated but fragile reflective mind faded out and the tough but moronic reactive mind took over, a significant change took place. The data received by the reactive mind is not stored in the standard data banks but in a special reactive data bank. The reflective mind cannot comprehend this data because it is not in its banks, and it has no access to the reactive bank. Even worse, it will reduce the effectiveness of its decisions. For some reason, this reactive data tends to disrupt and short circuit the standard banks; and the more there is of this reactive data, the more disruptive it becomes.

The reactive mind is a simple, tough mechanism that operates on a purely survival basis. That data, stored in its bank when it was in command, is mulled over by the reactive mind and it gets something like this out of the activity—"fire, blanket, hot, door, hot, fire, run, stairs, drop blanket." So Tom, not really knowing why, always sleeps with a heavy blanket on the foot of his bed and leaves the door to hall ajar. Now the reflective mind, on the other hand, if it knew of the data in the reactive banks, would demand fire escapes outside all fourth floor rooms.

Hubbard thinks the reactive mind is a holdover from

primitive times when survival situations occurred frequently, and
before languages were in use. With the advent of languages, and
particularly complex languages, the reactive mind becomes more
of a liability than an asset.

A way to illustrate this is to change the story about Tom just
a little. Say that he was burned slightly on the arm while running
down the burning hall and while still in pain (reflective mind
tuned out), was checked into the school's infirmary, where a
busy doctor and two nurses were helping more serious cases. The
dialogue in the room might sound something like this, "That arm
will never be the same again—he's had a shot; he will feel better
soon—don't touch that girl!"

Now, the reactive mind has just come thru a survival
situation, is still in command due to the pain, and takes literally
any commands or information given to it, particularly if they are
going to aid survival, and it *KNOWS* doctors and nurses can be
trusted to aid survival. Even though the doctor was talking about
some other person's arm, and Tom has but a small burn on his
arm, his arm may never be completely well again. This because
the reactive mind thought the doctor was talking about Tom's
arm. The power of the mind to retard healing is awesome.

"He's had a shot; he will feel better soon." Tom's reactive
mind relates a shot to drinking, and from then on will always
drink too much, in order to "feel better soon." "Don't touch that
girl" can make Tom uncomfortable when touching any girl for
the rest of his life.

Hubbard contends that an average person is functioning at
but a fraction of their potential due to these reactive mind
interpretations, called "engrams," generated during times of
either physical pain or painful emotion. In order to remove these
engrams and their detrimental effects from the reactive data
bank, *Dianetics* outlines a technique called reverie, a kind of
waking state hypnosis. In reverie, another person, called an
auditor, takes a person such as Tom back on a time track to the
time of the fire and allows the reflective to comprehend and
assimilate the whole episode and then store it in its own data
banks. The reactive mind will attempt in every way to conceal
the activity done while it was in command. But with skill and
perseverance, the reflective mind will finally comprehend by
actually reliving the incident, sometimes with a lot of the

emotion involved. At this time, the data is moved from the reactive to the standard data banks, and the engram will disappear.

When all the engrams are worked out, and none remain in the reactive data bank, the person becomes what is termed a "clear" in Dianetics; an individual operating at optimum efficiency, with no crossed circuitry causing irrational behavior.

Another interesting feature of the reactive mind that was discovered during sessions of reverie was it seems to function on a cellular level prior to birth, all the way back to the conception stage. According to Hubbard they have, thru reverie, recalled incidents involving physical pain when the person describing it was in the womb. This was down to recalling words said, actions taken, and outside noises heard, which were later verified by people other than the embryo involved.

Hubbard, in *Dianetics*, has described more accurately than Freud just how the mind functions. His assurance that any friend can become an auditor during reverie may be a little shaky, but he has corrected this in his updated version of Dianetics called Scientology; there specific training is required for each auditor before they are allowed to audit. In addition, levels of achievement above a clear have been established. The above brief description of Dianetics is not to be construed as an advertisement or endorsement of courses in Scientology—Dianetics is as stated; a fascinating and very plausible explanation of just how the mind really functions.

Another interesting look at aspects of the mind was made by Max Freedom Long, who wrote a series of books, the only one that comes to mind now is *The Secret Science Behind Miracles*, which deals with the priests, or kahunas, of old Hawaii. After living in Hawaii for years while searching for the secrets of the kahunas, Long finally admitted defeat and moved back to the mainland. He was afraid that so many of the old kahunas were dying without passing on their lore, their wisdom might be lost forever. He feared no one would ever know about their fire-walking, instant healing of broken bones, telepathy, and death-wishing. But one night, months later on the mainland, he awoke from a sound sleep with the answer—analyze the words used by the kahunas and see if they revealed any special meaning. The native Hawaiian words are made up of many two and three letter components, each of which may have several different meanings. By analyzing the words used to describe kahuna activity, Long was able to develop a general kahuna philosophy.

The kahunas believed that each person had three selves. The first was the middle self, which corresponds to the conscious mind, or the reflective mind of Dianetics. It runs the vehicle in the process of everyday living. The second was the lower self, similar to the subconscious mind, or the reactive mind of Dianetics. This is the one that expresses our emotion, does the astral traveling, and is our link with our Godhood. The third was our higher self, our Godhood, Devine Essence, or navigator. Incidentally, the kahunas gave a detailed description of the subconscious centuries before it was discovered by Freud.

The most interesting thing about the three selves was their working relationship. If the middle self wanted to accomplish some difficult task, it could enlist the aid of the lower self. This little rascal could do all sorts of feats. If telepathy was required, the lower self could go to distant points and observe people or activities there. This was done by the extension of so-called aka threads by the lower self. These threads were an extension of the invisible body of the lower self and could be extended instantly to distances of thousands of miles, as is done in what is called astral traveling in metaphysics. The lower self was considered to be a rather willful and spoiled child, who had to be humored or coerced into doing some action desired by the middle self. Prayer and fasting are efforts by the middle self to show the lower self that it (the middle self) is serious and needs help. It does appear, however, that the middle self of the kahunas had some sort of a hammer lock on their lower self; they seemed to be able to will the lower self into action with great certainty. Wouldn't it be nice to know their secret?

Many of the requests for aid made by the middle self to the lower self were requests for help from the higher self. This was because the middle self cannot contact the higher self directly, but most go thru the lower self.

Long relates instances when the kahunas performed instant healing of broken bones. The explanation of how it was done is, once again, intriguing (if you are tired of seeing the word intriguing, you may mentally substitute fascinating, astounding, or stimulating—but intriguing best fits the situation and describes the goal—to pique your imagination. And besides, the author *likes* the word intriguing. So you will see the word again and again. Please bear with one of many idiosyncrasies). According to the kahunas, each human has several bodies. The one we see is, of course, the physical body. Another one is the etheric body, which is supposed to occupy roughly the same area as the physical body. When a bone is broken in the physical body, say an ankle, the kahuna would grasp the ankle and hold it in the correct position and image in his mind a picture of a complete, unbroken etheric ankle. After about five minutes, according to witnesses at several of these events, the physical ankle was whole again, permitting the victim to walk. Kahunas are not the only ones who practice this art.

To demonstrate the power of the mind that can be generated by a kahuna, the use of the death wish will be examined. This also shows the corruption that power can develop thru centuries of use and that power is just that—power—and can be used for both good and evil.

The case cited by Long involved a boy from a remote village whose kahuna had forbidden anyone to work for the newly arrived white men. The boy was one of several hired by the curator of a museum for an archaeological trip to a mountain. While on the mountain, the boy lost the feeling in his feet and, realizing his kahuna had put the death wish on him, prepared himself to die. The curator knew a little bit about the death wish and recognized the symptoms. The kahuna had convinced his lower self of the wrongness of the boy's actions and had enlisted its aid in directing some disincarnated entities to the boy where they started to drain off the boy's vital force. This would result in the loss of feeling and the power of movement, first in the feet and then gradually working up, over a day or two, to the heart, at which time the victim would die.

The curator had heard only verbal descriptions of the death wish, but remembered that the kahuna usually built a mental guard around himself, just in case someone tried to turn those disincarnated entities around and send them back to rob his own vital force. The curator decided, correctly, that the kahuna might not have erected such a guard around himself, as he thought no one on the expedition knew very much about the death wish.

The curator began to perform. He extolled the virtues of the victim and assailed the character and motives of a kahuna who would want to harm such a fine boy. The curator was a tall man and, drawing himself up to his full height and speaking in a commanding voice, he ordered the entities to leave the boy and to go back and take care of that evil old kahuna. Shortly afterwards, the boy was able to move his feet.

The curator's curiosity got the better of him and he took the expedition back by way of the boy's village. When they arrived, no one was sight. The boy finally was able to coax his people out of the surrounding jungle. The villagers then told the curator that about the same time of day on the day the boy had regained the use of his feet, the kahuna had jumped up off of his mat and shouted, "Someone did it! Someone did it!"—and died the next day.

A very interesting book, *Kinship With All Life*, by J. Allen Boone, describes communication between humans and various animals. The author had been asked, decades ago, to take care of Strongheart, the famous German Shepherd of the silent movies. It quickly became an educational experience for the human, with the dog as the instructor. Boone learned that if we approach another animal on the basis of being equals, we can communicate. This is extremely difficult for humans to do as all of our relationships with animals are on a superior to inferior basis. We must get down to an eyeball to eyeball level to succeed. Once we do this, and mentally review the virtues and capabilities of whatever species we are trying to reach, and be sincere about it, we are preparing ourselves to communicate with them.

Humans, of all the animals, are the least able to perceive this universal mental language that we once used so well. Because they have concentrated so long and hard on oral means, they cannot receive what it is that the animals want to convey. Boone claims communication with dogs, flies, rattlesnakes, earthworms and horses.

One of the most unique relationships was claimed by a biologist, J.W. Jean, with his micro-organisms. Because of the communication and understanding between Jean and his brood, he was able to get results when his colleagues would fail, even when using the same formulas, equipment, and species.

An interesting aspect of this communication was the ability of animals to know the character of a stranger on sight. Boone tells of taking Strongheart into a lawyer's office. The lawyer, wanting to show the dog to his partner, took Boone and the dog into the next office, where the partner was talking to two men. The minute Strongheart entered the room, he growled and lunged at one of the two strangers, almost jerking the leash out of Boone's hand. After leaving the office, Boone asked the lawyer what he knew about the man. The lawyer didn't know the man well, but said he was a leading businessman and highly respected in the city. Weeks later, the man was exposed as one of the most dishonest big deal promoters in the country, and was later indicted. Boone devotes one chapter to what he calls nudists, emphasizing that our thoughts are much more noticeable than we imagine, particularly to animals. It appears to be a mental or thought impression rather than an observed aura interpretation.

There was a lecture given in Seattle years ago by a man from California whose name has been lost in the shuffle. He would communicate with dogs brought in by local people attending the lecture. One dog was memorable because of his insistence that the door to the back seat of the family car had something wrong with it, in spite of the owner's denial. Finally a friend of the owner stood up and said that the owner had never sat in the back seat of the car and there *was* something wrong with that door. Also a bit of trivia; dogs, at least in Seattle, consider one of the human years to be two of theirs, with one year for the winter and one for the summer (now, we are very familiar with Seattle weather, and sometimes WE think of winter as being a year by itself! Maybe in San Diego, a dog's year is the same as a human's).

One eye-opening discovery which seems to involve the use of the mind is the Hieronymus machine (here again, that is *about* the right spelling. There are many advantages to living in a small town, as the author does. But a major disadvantage is the absence of adequate library facilities). This is an electronic box that has been put to commercial use in the United States, primarily for the control of pests in crops. A company in California takes aerial photos of thousands of acres of crops which have been infested with either insects or fungi. The areas of infestation are circled on the negative, and then the negative is attached to a coil on top of the machine. When the power is turned on, a person who is trained to operate the machine mentally directs that the cause of the blight on the circled crops be eliminated. Within a day or two the pests, whether bores, beetles, or fungi, or whatever, are dead. The method must be successful, as thousands of acres have been treated in the past in California, Pennsylvania, and Florida.

An unusual thing about this phenomena is the selectivity that can be obtained. In one photo, with ten rows of infested corn, rows 1, 3, 5, 7, and 9 were circled and treated with the machine. The following day, dead corn bores were found in rows 1, 3, 5, 7, and 9 while the bores were busy eating rows 2, 4, 6, 8, and 10.

One operator was reported to have experimented with the box and discovered an astounding fact—the machine would function without being plugged into electric power. Experimenting further, he found that although it would function without power, it would not work if any of the tubes or the crystal were removed. Then, as the ultimate test, he states that he sketched a diagram of the box, and when all the proper components were in their right place, and he placed a marked negative on the diagram and mentally directed action to occur, he got the proper results! (Now, this we would all have to see to believe!). But the author knows of this machine being used to eliminate viruses in humans. It would appear, if this experiment did occur and was successful, that the machine serves as either a catalyst or an amplifier of the mental processes of certain humans.

This machine is another good example of power possibly being used for both good and evil. The above-mentioned article hinted at the mysterious deaths of many of the people doing research with this machine and a possible race with the USSR in this new field of psionics, or psychically operated devices. Boy, does that sound out of date! By now, probably 95% of Americans believe that Communism is dead and we haven't a worry in the world about the nuclear and other weapons still in Russian hands. The author certainly hopes the majority is right, but it brings to mind that old sports saying—It aint over till its over!

But back to reality. It is rumored that this machine can be used to locate a person whose photo is placed in the coil. And if it can kill bugs and fungi at a distance of many miles, immediately the question comes to mind—could it kill a human?

For good or evil, for better or worse, this machine is here and we had better find out how it works.

One things is certain—A reader of the records such as Mark is able to locate anyone living on Earth at this time. When Mark is asked, while in a self-induced trance, the location of a particular person on this Earth, he says it is like looking up at a sky filled with millions of stars. Suddenly one star stands out, brighter than all the rest and with this clue, he can describe where the person is at that moment, what the person is currently doing, describe him physically as though looking at a fluoroscope, and describe in detail the person's past lives and karmic relationships.

Indeed, this computer each one of us carries between our ears is a truly marvelous instrument about which we know very little.

THE BODY

The vehicle for our souls here on this fifth plane planet, our good old Mother Earth, is the physical body of Homo Sapiens, which is both our joy and our sorrow. The joy is the experiences brought in thru our five senses; the sight of a beautiful mountain scene, the sound of the roaring surf, the taste of fine wine, the smell of a gardenia, the feel of the touch of a loved one. These same senses can just as easily bring sorrow; partial or total loss of the first four senses, and the increase in feeling when pain occurs. Pain from arthritis, pain from bad teeth, pain from injured backs—the list seems endless.

Primitive man, as well as animals, seem less inflicted with illness than modern man, but this may be an illusion. The primitive man who survived childhood was the exception. Old age was a luxury attained by but a few, as life expectancy was about half that of modern man. Pain was a way of life in primitive societies; it was tolerated and respected.

Modern humans have special problems; they live longer and the vehicle simply wears out. They eat too much food detrimental to their health, they exercise too little, and they pollute their own and other people's lungs with smoke.

These modern humans have the advantage of an advanced technology to help cure the ailments of their physical bodies. Polio, smallpox, cholera, and many others diseases have been all but eliminated. Even worn out organs are being replaced. Each new week brings new surgical techniques that accomplish truly fantastic things.

Yet with all the technology at their command, the modern doctors cannot heal as Jesus did. Many people will use the miracles of the Bible to prove the divinity of Jesus and the mortalness of humans. It should be remembered, however, that the disciples of Jesus also healed, thus proving that it was a learning process.

Today, miraculous cures are being accomplished all over the world. Probably the most publicized and debated healing is the psychic surgery being done in the Philippines and Brazil. These healers, using only their bare hands, are able to make incisions into the body. After correcting a function or removing cancerous material, the incision is closed without leaving a scar. Another interesting aspect of this surgery is that there is no infection, even though the operations are often times done under very unclean conditions.

There has been much controversy, right up to the present time, on the subject of psychic surgery, with doctors and the American Medical Association on one side, and the people cured and their travel agents who sent them on the other side. Some reports of animal blood being found on towels used to wipe off patients after surgery gave rise to speculation that there was no opening of the body at all. Because of all this controversy, Mark was asked to do some readings on the subject about 15 years ago. The readings stated that the psychic surgery was superior to modern western techniques. The hands and arms of the healer are in a trance state, and the power in one hand causes the molecules in the patient's flesh to repel each other when the healer's fingers are drawn along the patient's skin. It also causes impurities in the system to collect in the area of the incision for removal, as well as somehow preventing any infection. When the other hand is removed from alongside the incision, the area is restored to the condition as it was before the incision was made.

The readings (August 1974) state that approximately 27% of the Americans going to the Philippines at that time for psychic surgery were being treated by genuine psychic healers, such as Tony Agpaoa. Another 20% were being treated by healers with lesser but still considerable healing ability. The other 53% ranged from laying on of the hands, some good at it, down to the animal blood tricks. There is a terrific demand for psychic surgeons so, by golly, we will give them psychic surgeons!

Some interesting results have come out of tests conducted by a Japanese doctor, as described in the book, *Psychic Surgery In The Philippines*. One test was a measurement of the brain waves of a psychic healer while operating. Electrodes from a recorder were attached to the healer's head. The machine registered normal brain waves until the healer started to open. At that time, the stylus on the recorder proceeded to run right up off the graph paper, at which time the machine stopped working, and did not function again until completely overhauled back in Japan.

Another incident was related by Nelson Decker, a chiropractor who had worked for several months with the healers in the Philippines, first with the Espiritista Church healers and then with Tony Agpaoa, probably the most famous of the healers. After assisting Tony for a period with chiropractic treatments, Nelson was told by Tony that the Holy Spirit had said Nelson was ready to learn how to perform the psychic surgery. Tony said for the first lesson, he would put Nelson completely into a trance, which he did—he blew in Nelson's ear.

Nelson said he could feel nothing and was hardly able to open his eyes in order to walk stiffly to the table with the patient on it. He would struggle to open his eyes occasionally to see his hands working busily inside the patient's body. He had no control over his hands at all.

The following day, Tony put only Nelson's hands and arms into the trance. Nelson walked over to the patient and his hands opened the abdomen and started operating inside the body. After a time, the thought flashed through Nelson's mind, "What am I doing here in the Philippines with my hands inside someone's body doing things I know nothing about?"

The very second he had the thought, Nelson saw his hands stop moving. Immediately Tony, who had been standing with his back towards Nelson while working on another patient, turned towards Nelson and said, "Think about anything else but what you are thinking right now. Think about a cold beer."

Nelson thought of a cold beer and his hands started moving again.

Nelson was told by Tony that if he would stay in the Philippines for two more years, he would be able to do the surgery on his own. Soon afterwards, however, Nelson left the Philippines but he thought, at the time of the lecture in 1974, that he would be able to put his own arms and hands in a trance-state and do the psychic surgery when he reached a certain level of spiritual development. The author has not heard from Nelson in over a decade.

Although psychic surgery leaves no scar, Nelson told of one healer looking at a man's back and stating that other psychic healers had worked on this man. When Nelson asked the healer how he could tell, the healer passed his hand over the back and faint red lines appeared on the skin. The healer pointed to one line and said, "Tony operated there, but I don't know about that one or that one."

He then operated successfully. In about four hours, the red lines disappeared.

One may ask why repeated operations are needed, if psychic surgery is such a good thing. Psychic surgery is just a surgical technique. Although superior to western surgery, if the things that caused the problem in the first place are not corrected, the condition can return. Bad diet, stress, physical strain, or another malfunctioning organ can cause the same problem to reoccur.

Psychic surgery was founded in the Philippines by a man (you are right! I can't find the man's name in my notes) who was executed by the Spanish rulers in the 19th century. The Espiritista Church later split off from the Catholic Church because of their healing practices. They are always on the lookout for potential healers in their congregation, and in the mid 1970s claimed to have about 35 healers.

The most famous healer, Tony Agpaoa, does not work with the Espiritista healers but at the age of nine, was told in a vision that he would become a healer. As part of his training, he was told to go out in the jungle for three weeks and practice developing his power of concentration. At the end of three weeks, he could select and concentrate on one particular coconut at the top of a tall tree, point his finger a the coconut, and it would fall to the ground.

Nelson wrote of another incident when he and Tony were eating lunch in a fly-infested room. A truck driver came in, complaining of a pain in the abdomen. Tony wiped his hands on a rag, opened the man's abdomen, and discovered a section of diseased intestine. Tony had Nelson get a pair of old rusty scissors and cut one end of the diseased section. Tony cut the other end with his bare finger. Holding the two severed ends together, he ran his finger around the joint, much as you would braze the ends of two copper pipes. The two ends were permanently joined together. Tony then stuffed the intestines back in place and closed the abdomen. The truck driver gave Tony a small amount of money, pulled up his pants, and went back to work. Tony and Nelson wiped off their hands and finished their lunch.

Nelson told of a field trip with healers to the town of Batangas, south of Manila, where the healers treated hundreds of people in one day. Women would line up for the removal of diseased ovaries. It was done on a door placed on two saw horses. Nelson timed several of these operations and found that from the time a woman's feet left the ground, she stretched out on the door, the healer opened, removed the ovaries, and closed, and the woman's feet hit the ground on the other side of the door, averaged 25 seconds.

In another incident, the author and his wife watched a home movie on psychic surgery and later talked at length with the couple who produced the film. At that time, the husband was an airline pilot, who had earlier been increasingly hampered by a calcified growth on the back of one hand, the result of an old injury. After X-raying his hand, his own doctor said he could operate and remove the growth, but it would keep the pilot from flying for some time. As he was flying the Manila run at the time, the pilot looked up the healers and asked if they could remove the growth without a lot of "down" time. Their answer was "no problem." As the pilot is a very methodical person, he delayed having it done until the next trip, taking his wife along to document the operation, as she owned and operated a photographic shop. He returned home and confronted his doctor and had another X-ray taken of his hand. The doctor compared the two X-rays, and stammered that it was impossible; he must have gotten the old X-rays mixed up with some others.

The pilot related a later incident when his healer, along with two other healers, stayed at his home for three days, a stopover on their way to Washington, D.C. The healers asked the pilot if he didn't know of anyone needing to be healed during their stay. As the pilot was a trustee in his church, word quietly got around about the healers, and by the third day, two ministers and the head of the Jesuit order had funneled several hundred people into the pilot's basement for treatment. On the last day, a neighbor of the pilot called the police station, complaining of an orgy doing on next door, with people going in and out all hours of the day and night. The police detective answering the phone, who normally was nowhere near that phone, reassured the caller that the police knew all about the event, that it was a church retreat and would end that day. The detective had been one of those hundreds who had been treated.

The last incident told by the pilot involved a diplomat at the Philippine Embassy in Washington, D.C. A very difficult operation had to be performed and the diplomat had his own surgeon flown over from the Philippines. What was surprising was that he had a woman psychic healer flown over as well. He then told the surgeon to operate but if the healer was to give any instructions, he was to do what she said. The surgeon had never worked with a healer before and didn't want to work under those conditions, but the diplomat was adamant. The surgeon finally reluctantly agreed, and operated with the healer right at his side. The operation was a complete success, and even the surgeon admitted that part of the credit had to go to the advice of the healer.

The reaction of the medical profession is understandable. For untrained people, some with only a grade school education, to accomplish a feat that a medical doctor cannot do, even with 20 years of intense training and backed by very advanced technology, is unthinkable.

Probably the best illustration of this reaction is described in the book, *Psychic Surgery in the Philippines*. An older doctor (in the absence of a name, we will call him Dr. Doe), known as a skilled diagostician, had accompanied the author of the book to the Philippines to witness and either verify or refute an actual demonstration of psychic surgery. Finally it happened. Dr. Doe stood across the table from Tony Agpaoa as the healer opened a patient with his bare hands. Tony requested Doe to put his hands in the opening to assure himself that there was indeed, an opening. Doe refused the offer. At the conclusion of the operation, after Tony had closed the opening without leaving a scar, Tony offered Doe a can containing the cancerous material from the patient, asking him to test both the blood of the patient and the material in the can to make sure it was the same. Doe refused, and practically ran from the room. Later, back in the United States, Doe stated on national T.V. that he thought the whole thing was a fake, and that it had looked like animal blood. The truth is his well-trained mind refused to believe his eyes!

One last incident on psychic surgery was related by Nelson to the author after one of his lectures. He described a later trip to the Philippines with a photographer from NASA. Nelson did not know exactly what NASA had in mind, but they appeared to be interested to see if a genuine healer could operate on demand; that is, not with a lot of excuses as to why he couldn't operate on a moments notice.

The photographer was setting up his equipment to document Tony opening a patient. Tony thought the photographer was ready to take picture so he opened the patient. Nelson then told Tony the photographer wasn't ready, so Tony just zipped up the patient and stood waiting. The photographer was so excited he could hardly finish setting up his equipment. He kept on exclaiming, "He did it! He did it! He really can open!"

Nelson claims to have tried to find out what were NASA's conclusions about Tony, but all they would say is that they thought it was a real phenomena.

It is sad that doctors and the AMA take such a negative attitude towards psychic surgery. One would think they would at least conduct one complete study of a well-known healer such as Tony, with complete lab analysis by a well supervised team, and by doing so live up to their Hippocratic Oath, which states that they will use every means available to cure their patients. But the author doesn't think that it will be done in the near future—the medical profession refuses to admit that psychic surgery could be a valid technique. Actually they really feel threatened by this phenomena which they cannot explain or understand. With two doctors in the immediate family, the author is very familiar with the mindset of the medical profession.

Two decades ago a French doctor, Leboyer (we think that is the right spelling), advocated a new and exciting technique at childbirth. He believed the occasion should be a calm and peaceful event, rather than the traumatic production we make of it today. Extreme care was taken to make the conditions of the womb and room as similar as possible. The room was kept in semi-darkness and no talking was allowed. The infant was held and massaged constantly after birth. It was placed in water for a while, simulating the environment of the womb. Only as a last resort was the baby hung by the heels and slapped on the bottom.

Normal pain at birth is normally multiplied by many factors. How would *you* like to be pulled from a nice, warm, wet, quiet, dark world where you had been growing for months, and then be extruded into a glaring, noisy world? Added to the screaming of a mother in pain, think of being hung up by the heels and spanked! If we ever had an intuitive thought, it was after seeing films of Leboyer and his techniques with infants at birth. You immediately say to yourself, "That is right—why have we been doing it so wrong for so long." Remember Dianetics and engrams caused by physical pain? Think of how many engrams are caused in a chatty delivery room.

Along the same lines as Leboyer's approach is that of Dr. Murooka in Tokyo, who made a recording of the sounds in a womb. Playing the recording had an immediate soothing effect. Tested on 500 infants, it stopped almost all from crying. On the average, it required only 34 seconds of the recording to stop a new born baby from crying.

We are getting to know quite a bit about the vehicle for fifth plane souls on planet Earth, but there is more information out there not yet discovered or utilized that would allow us to get more miles out of the old vehicle, and more importantly, with more comfort. Besides the normal precaution of using only good clean fuel, we should look at the danger of some of the fuel additives, damage caused by too much smoke in the air intake, and the impact of too many high speed runs. Working on better repairs for the exhaust system should get a high priority. We should find out just how many mechanical breakdowns are in reality caused by a malfunctioning on-board computer. And someone should certainly solve the problem of rocks getting into the ball joints and making them stiff. Many of our senior citizens, the author included, know all about that problem!

POLITICS

All work and no play is a bore, so it has been decided to inject a little humor into this tome, and what better object for humor could be found than politics, or more specifically, politicians. The reader should be warned, however, that very treacherous ground is being explored—the youngest son, an overseas school administrator, after reading a rough draft of this chapter, said to leave this chapter out of the book. He said no publisher would accept the book with this chapter in it. So you may never read this chapter.

But this far along in the book, maybe politics is just another windmill for Don Quixote's lance, so it has been decided to proceed. If you read this chapter, and find any smudged letters, it may be the publisher's tears for printing it. Brace yourself!

When anyone discusses politics, veins stand out on necks, spleens are vented, and all kinds of ruckuses take place. Now, our goal should be to remain calm and objective while considering this topic. The only way one can be objective is to stand 'way back and look at some other people's political setup and problems.

Well, there is a small star, about six inches to the left of the North Star, that has a planet named ARAT in orbit around it that is very similar to our Earth. Why, it has two superpowers distrustful of each other. One is called US and the other is called THEM. We will look at US first because it has two political parties just like the United States. One calls themselves Asses, but as ladies down here reading this book might be offended, we will call them Spendocrats. They are aptly named; they love to spend money. Whenever they are voted into office, they borrow money and ladle it out like the stuff was going out of style.

The other major party is called POGs—that stands for Profit On Groans. They believe everyone should work hard, save their money and invest it, and then live happily ever after on the interest. In that way, the government wouldn't have to borrow and ladle out any money at all; maybe just deliver the mail. But they would have to keep enough slingshots and spears handy to make sure that pesky country THEM wouldn't dare start anything.

So, in good times, when people had lots of principal and

interest, they voted in the POGs. When times got tough, and even nickels were hard to come by, they would vote in the Spendocrats, who would start ladling out the money again.

It went on for decades. First one party in and then the other, until finally the BIG HARD TIMES came along. Why, you couldn't even find pennies! Well, sure 'nough, the Spendocrats were voted in and they put away their ladles and got out their shovels and moved so much borrowed money out that just about everybody got splashed by it. Then they learned a surprising truth—if they splashed enough borrowed money on enough people, the Spendocrats would be voted in even in good times! This is because of what they call animal nature up there; we call it human nature down here.

Up to this point, the government of US had prided itself on treating each citizen the same, and before the BIG HARD TIMES that was true—they didn't give them much of anything! Even the Spendocrats had ladled it out both evenly and sparingly. But after the BIG HARD TIMES, the Spendocrats were shoveling so hard that a fella could stand in one place and be splashed by the shovelfuls from different shovelers.

Then the Spendocrats ran pipelines to everyone's house so it was hard to tell who got how much. People would look at their neighbors and wonder how much they had been splashed. Pressure groups began to form to get more of the money for themselves. The tillers of the soil, the milkers of the cows, the keepers of the slingshots, the workers in the sweat shops, and the rear end sitters (our equivalent of welfare)—each one trying to get their snout deeper into the government trough.

Before the BIG HARD TIMES, everyone KNEW if they didn't work hard, save their money, and have kids to take care of them in their old age, they would starve to death. So they WORKED, and WORKED HARD! But when the Spendocrats started shoveling money into the pipelines to the rear end sitters, animal nature took over. Rear end sitters became the fastest growing segment of the population.

One of the biggest programs for rear end sitters up there was called SKIBUM. It had another name but everyone called it SKIBUM, which stands for *S*hovelfuls to *K*eep on *I*ncreasing *B*abies and *U*nwed *M*others. The Spendocrats had shoveled so many whizbangs (that is the equivalent of a dollar down here) into this program that folks didn't dare loiter outside of a SKIBUM office or they would get trampled underfoot by the junior high and high school dropouts coming in to sign up. It was the best pay a poor, single, female, teenage dropout could find. And guess where these dropouts had heard about SKIBUM? From their mothers, who had lived all their lives on SKIBUM, who had heard it from their mothers, who had lived all their lives on SKIBUM, who had—boy, did it ever change the meaning of the word family in US. About half of the children born in the major cities of US were born out of wedlock. And it proves something else—the stronger and more comfortable you build a crutch, the more cripples you will create.

Now there are two bodies of lawmakers in this country called US. One was called the Toastmasters and was regarded as sort of a debating society. This was because every few years the control swung to the other party and, because of this frequent change of leadership, it didn't have have a lot of power. The other body was called the House, but the Spendocrats had been in power there for so long they called it Home. They had the real control over how much money to tax and borrow and how it would be spent.

A few years back, a funny thing started to happen. The people would vote the Spendocrats into the Home and the Toastmasters, to make sure the whizbangs would keep coming their way, but they would vote in a POG as leader, because the POGs were the only ones who knew how to run things and keep a wary eye on THEM. The people knew the Spendocrats were only good at shoveling out money.

After a few decades, the Spendocrats had a problem. They had borrowed so many whizbangs that a big chunk of the budget had to be used just to pay the interest on the growing debt. Even some of the people getting splashed began to yell about the size of the debt. So the Spendocrats did two things. The first was to shift the blame for the debt from themselves to the POG leader, who was called the High Muckimuck. Now, this takes some doing, because the only ones authorized to levy taxes or borrow money and then allocate it in US are joint actions by the Toastmasters and the Home. They shifted the blame by what they call the "BIG FIB" up there—say something long enough and loud enough and people will believe it. They kept on harping on the "High Muckimuck deficit" until everybody believed it. The second thing they did was to cut back on the spears and the slingshots.

The Spendocrats had an ally in this latter effort. The High Muckimuck of THEM was a crafty character who said, "Let's have peace—let's cut back on arms." He threw away a lot of old spears and made a deal with US to get rid of all the boomerangs, a nice little weapon you could send out close to the ground so it could hit you in the back of the head before you could turn around.

In the wide open society of US, everyone knew that US had made only 300 boomerangs, and all 300 were to be destroyed. But in the closed society of THEM, when they said they were going to destroy all 600 of their boomerangs, who was to know if that was all they had made? The best guess of the US spearthrowers was that THEM had built at least *900*! To allay the US fears, the High Muckimuck of THEM issued an invitation. "You-all come on over, bring your marshmallows, and we will have a picnic while we watch the boomerangs burn. We will get them all together at the woodshop where they were built and we will sit and watch all 600 burn. In fact, we will let you stand on the roof of the woodshop and you can look for as far as you can see."

Just to give you some idea, THEM is the largest country on ARAT. It is about 8 million hourwalks in area (an hourwalk is the area an average man can walk around in one hour, or about one square mile). That leaves about 7,999,900 hourwalks unobserved. Boy, you can sure hide a lot of little boomerangs in 7,999,900 hourwalks!

Now a lot of THEM's allies, and even THEM themselves, are in the process of converting from oligarchic to democratic governments, and peace is in the air. But the spearthrowers and hardliners in THEM are still a potent force. They still have their hands on the spears. The best seer on ARAT, when asked when the next global war would occur, said he thought at the latest by 1996. Now everyone *knows* US wouldn't start a global war, so there are two possibilities. The first is that the THEM High Muckimuck is pulling a fast one; that all of his talk of peace is just a smoke screen to make US drop their guard. But he *looks* and *sounds* so peaceful. Golly, you can even see where the dove of peace sat on his bald head and unloaded! But some people think that bear hug of friendship might be fatal. The other possibility is that the spearthrowers of THEM will get so mad at their peace-loving leader that they will throw him out within 6 years and put in their own High Muckimuck. Then they will do what they have wanted to do all along—keep on trying to expand THEM's control over all of ARAT.

Don't worry about a global war. It's up to THEM and they will start one when they get good and ready. All US can do is to keep their spears and slingshots ready, and not go overboard on a "peace dividend." (One remote third possibility exists—up on ARAT, they have some crazies much like the Middle East crazies we have down here on Earth. They are beginning to get some pretty good spears, and might try throwing a few at US but make it look like the spears came from THEM, or even vice versa. These crazies are crazy enough to think that if they could provoke a war between US and THEM, they might be able to pick up the pieces after US and THEM finish tearing each other apart.)

Instead, some people in US think they should be working on that pesky deficit. There is a problem the High Muckimuck, the Toastmasters, and the Home could try to solve if they really tried. They might say NO to the special interest groups. No more whizbangs to the tillers of the soil; the billions already given to them have made them less efficient, thus losing foreign markets and hitting the US taxpayers two ways—higher food prices and higher taxes. And the same for the milkers of the cows. No more millions of whizbangs a month to store thousands of tons of refrigerated high cholesterol stuff to give to school kids and rear end sitters, who shouldn't be eating it anyway. No siree!

You may ask will they get together and do it? Well, as long as the Spendocrats control both the Toastmasters and the Home——CAN TURTLES FLY??? The Spendocrats have the technique of splashing money around down to an art, and they have splashed so many people that animal nature has set in. It is awfully hard to vote them out of the Toastmasters and particularly the Home because if the POGs get in, they won't splash as much money—right? So the beings on ARAT are finding out just what we have learned down here on Earth; in free elections, the legislative bodies you get are just exactly what you vote into office. And animal nature up there appears to be very similar to human nature down here.

With this rather brief look at the political process on ARAT, we should be able to look at our own political problems here on Earth with great objectivity—right? How much have *YOU* been splashed lately and how are *YOU* going to vote in the next election?

Now that you have finished reading this chapter, how do you feel about it? Should it be left in the book or should it be thrown out? Let's have a vote on the subject, a real consensus of opinion, the basis of a little conventional wisdom of our own. Cast your vote!

Leave it in   __________
throw it out   __________
publisher's comments   __________

WHY ARE WE HERE AND WHERE DO WE GO FROM HERE?

The man on the bed was dying. His breathing was shallow and faint. The bed rested on a large set of scales in a sealed room. Two men watched the dying man thru a window in the room and monitored life support equipment; pulse rate, respiration, blood pressure, etc. To one side, a stylus moved on a roll of graph paper, recording the combined weight of both the man and the bed with accuracy down to grams.

Suddenly, one of the observer's spoke, "He is failing fast. Look at that irregular heart beat!"

Tensely, they hunched over the instruments. All at once, they both started talking.

"Did you see that!"

"I can't believe it!"

"Right after the heart stopped!"

A scene such as this actually occurred and then was repeated many times as these two men (our notes do not even have an initial, much less a name) set out to prove that there really is some physical evidence of the soul leaving the body at the instant of death, when the body lost a few grams of weight. Other than this test, we must rely on less physical evidence that a soul really exists. And that is what this chapter is all about—the soul. The chapter on where did we come from dealt with the vehicular part of human beings. Now we will shift gears in order to find out *WHY* we are here. It will be as though we are dealing with the driver rather than the vehicle. And they are different as night and day.

When we humans trace our ancestry, we automatically think about Mom and Dad, and the two Grammas and Grampas, etc. But that is just the vehicular, or mechanical side of the picture. In this great human race, even more important than the car is the Andretti, the Unser, and the Petty. That's right—the driver.

In an earlier chapter, we visualized drivers racing in heats of the human race, with a different vehicle in each heat. Each heat is a separate one act play. We actors zip ourselves into our vehicle, or costume, and interact with other actors, whom we are preordained to meet in this little one act play, one of many in which we take part. Although our meeting is preordained, our actions in the play are a matter of free will.

But we are getting ahead of ourselves. Let us look at what others say about souls. The Bible says that God created Man in his own image and likeness and after death, the soul goes to either Heaven or Hell and stays there for eternity. The Catholic Church adds an interim place, just after death, called Purgatory, where the souls rids itself of the earthly dross before going on to either Heaven or Hell.

Another source of information which also has a purgatory-like state is Theosophy, a late 19th century school of thought originated by Mde. H.P. Blavatsky. In her book, *The Secret Doctrine*, she describes in great detail the functions of the human soul, or Manas, and its relationship to the spirit, or Atmas. Although Theosophy is considered passe by many, and its libraries are usually tended and used by octogenarians, parts of it are worth quoting.

First, a bit of basic theosophical belief, quoting from *The Ocean of Theosophy*, written by W.Q. Judge, in 1891. This little book boils the almost unreadable tome of Blavasky down into understandable terms. Judge states, "that man possesses an immortal soul is the common belief of humanity; to this Theosophy adds that he *IS* a soul; and further that all nature is capable of sensation and consciousness, that the vast array of objects and man are not mere collections of atoms fortuitously thrown together and thus without law evolving law, but down to the smallest atom, all is soul and spirit, ever evolving under the rule of law which is inherent in the whole. And just as the ancients taught, so does Theosophy; that the source of evolution is the drama of the soul and that nature exists for no other purpose than the soul's experience."

Theosophy teaches that after death, the soul, the spirit, and the astral shell of a human leave the physical body and enter a purgatory-like state called Kama Loca. The soul and the spirit pass on after only a short stop, but the astral shell stays much longer, clinging as it does to the passions and earthly desires. It rids itself of these items reluctantly, appearing at seances and through mediums. It is not the soul or the spirit, but because of its involvement with them in the past life, it knows about that life and is often mistaken for the soul and the spirit. In some cases, these astral shells will last for some time; this is usually in the case of a very materialistic person or one very attached to someone still on Earth. They finally disintegrate and fade away.

Meanwhile, the soul and the spirit, after leaving the astral shell behind, enter the western equivalent of Heaven, Devacan, where the experiences and lessons of the life just completed are assimilated into the experiences of all the previous lifetimes. When this task is completed, the soul develops a desire to reincarnate. The soul then analyzes its worst Karmas that can be worked on in the near future. It will then choose a human body that will, in the future, come in association with other bodies whose souls have generated Karma in the past with which it now must meet in order to work out that Karma. As the soul enters the chosen body around the time of birth, it loses the memory of both Devacan and all previous incarnations.

Our next concept of the soul is that given by Edgar Cayce. This man was born in Kentucky in the 1880s and had very little formal education. As a young boy, Cayce read the Bible thru once for each year of his life, praying constantly for the power to help sick and ailing people. Finally, as a young man, he was given this power.

After years of the physical feelings, he finally was asked some philosophical questions and in answering them, Cayce introduced a new dimension to his work—he confirmed the theory of reincarnation. About 2500 of his readings are these so-called life readings. When given a name, birth place, and birth date, he could give the best vocational potentials of even babies at birth, based on a review of experiences in previous lifetimes. He could also give the prime Karmas to be worked out in this lifetime, Karma being the ancient law of cause and effect. "As ye sow, so shall ye reap." Every thought and every action generates an equal reaction. Beneficial thoughts and actions result in spiritual growth and detrimental thoughts and actions will have to be corrected, if not in this lifetime, in some future lifetime.

As an example, a man in ancient Persia held a position in the tribe that required him to burn out the eyes of all male prisoners captured in battle. He was born blind in the 20th century, not because of his job in ancient Persia, but because he *took pleasure* in performing the task!

The validity of the readings in more concrete areas, such as the physicals, is surprisingly accurate. Even forgetting the superhuman nature of the readings (from thousands of miles away and fluoroscopic vision of the body), his percentage of successes was excellent. If he proved accurate with his superhuman powers on a subject which can be easily proved or disproved, it lends credence to his work on less concrete subjects.

The philosophy that emerged from Cayce's readings (remember that he could remember almost nothing of what he uttered while in a trance) states that when the Universe was formed, all the souls were sent out from God to gain experience, and after countless experiences, to return to God. At first, because they had been with God, their total thoughts and actions paralleled God's, but gradually, as they gained experience, their paths diverged from that of God's, and they began to build or use physical forms and immense themselves in matter. Some of them finally reached the point of requiring a physical form in which to live. The law of Karma, which is actually the first or basic law, came into operation to enable those souls enmeshed in matter to find, thru many, many experiences, the way back so that their thinking once again paralleled God's thinking, at which time they would return to God.

In connection with the concept of the soul and reincarnation, Cayce said Man was a soul with a body as a vehicle; that the existence and decisions made by each human on this Earth are important, purposeful, and will effect that soul's future course; that it is not dust to dust for the soul, but only the body; that a soul's station in life, worldly possessions, race, sex, or intelligence have nothing to do with the spiritual status which is the most important status of all; that although the circumstances under which each soul enters this life are preordained, the extend to which each soul can then change these circumstances is almost limitless; that transmigration of souls (souls in human bodies later incarnating in animal bodies as a punishment) does not occur but that souls do progress from lower to higher animal forms.

The next source of information on the soul is our friend Mark, who had been taught how to do the Cayce type readings after both he and the author had a chance meeting with a stranger at a Theosophy meeting. The author was told by the stranger, after a few training sessions, that his conscious mind so dominated his subconscious mind that it would take years of training, time that neither the stranger nor the author had to spend. Mark, on the other hand, learned in a few weeks to go into a self-induced trance and contact the Cosmic and Akashic Records, as Cayce had done. The Akashic were best for general and philosophical questions while the Cosmic were best for details. As stated earlier, these records include every action and thought of every lifetime of every soul that had ever lived on this Earth.

The first task to be performed was a check to see if the information received from Mark agreed with that received from his teacher and from Cayce. Except for prophecy, in which there were differences on all sides, there was only one basic discrepancy between Mark and Cayce. This was on the subject of the Immaculate Conception, in that Cayce declared that it was true, but Mark said that it was intended as a teaching aid, but was not true.

One very interesting incident, showing a cross-tie between Mark and Cayce, was a reading by Mark for a man with a brain tumor, who had been given 6 months to live by 5 specialists. The man had lost the sight in one eye and was in intense pain, sleeping only two hours a night (he refused to take drugs for the relief of pain). The reading indicated that cryosurgery (local freezing of the area) would come closest to being successful, but would still leave him a vegetable. When asked who was the best neurosurgeon to contact, an out-of-state doctor was named. Then the reading volunteered that these two should meet, because in a previous incarnation in Arabia, the current patient had saved the current doctor's life, by removing a tumor from his leg.

Three weeks later, the out-of-state doctor came to town and visited his old friend, the patient's doctor. The visitor asked his friend if there were any interesting cases and was handed the patient's folder, which included a copy of the reading.

The doctor said the next day he had stayed up till 4 A.M. reviewing the case, but concluded that the reading was correct; he could get within 1/4 of an inch of the tumor but could not operate. It would severely damage the patient's brain and possibly kill him if the tumor was removed. He then told the local doctor an astounding thing. While in medical school, planning to be a general practitioner, he had been given a reading by Edgar Cayce in which he was told he should become a neurosurgeon because by doing so, he would be in a position to repay a debt to a man who had saved his life, in a previous incarnation in Arabia, by removing a tumor from his leg. The medical student decided to become a neurosurgeon.

The ideal ending to this story would be to have the surgeon perfect his technique and save the patient's life, but this was not to be. The tumor went into remission, the patient regained the sight in the blind eye and as of eight years later, when he moved away at the age of 68, was in good health.

One possible cause of the reversal was in the same reading. It stated that he had chosen an imperfect body in which to incarnate in this lifetime as a means of absorbing pain and suffering. This was to atone for a mistake he had made in the last lifetime. As the head of a monastery in Tibet, he had attempted, prematurely, to become an Ascended Master—and had failed (Jesus of Nazareth was an Ascended Master)! He had demanded and received a body in this lifetime in which he could experience intense pain and suffering. The reading advised him that his wish for atonement did not aid him spiritually.

A follow-up reading, taken a month later, stated, "(the patient) presently suffers a great confusion. Things are not as he thought they were. His black and white world is now many shades of gray, which is confusing to him. The impression here is an emergence and a denying of the emergence. The Entity here approaches the condition where he could set aside the subconscious demand for atonement, but at present is still learning to read the shades of gray. This is an evolutionary process, the lessons here of considerable benefit to the progress of the Entity, in that they have been avoided."

Thru Mark's gift, and the author was not the only one to use the gift, readings were done in a wide area of interests. While researching in one area, it was stated that it would not be detrimental to assist a mountain rescue unit in locating lost hunters and hikers. This effort was disappointing, and was discontinued after two readings. The first attempt located the wrong hunter. The second attempt pin-pointed the hunter but when the key question was asked—should a team go in a get him, the answer was no; for the first time, the man was thinking about his wife and three children and this whole situation had been set up to literally open his eyes.

At the end of that reading, the following information was

volunteered. "Information concerning individuals not present and who are lost, strayed, in locations unknown to those present, is of no value in the readings. The avowed purpose of these readings is spiritual development and spiritual growth of these Entities. If the information given is of no benefit to the seeker, it will not necessarily be correct. The information needed by the seeker (for spiritual growth) will be given and will be correct."

The following are some of the questions and answers taken from the readings concerning the soul:

Q. Is God, or the Source, or the Primemover, or the Deity the sum total of the spirit of all the souls, or centers of consciousness?

A. Essentially yes. This terminology is sufficient for the comprehension of the seeker.

Q. How was the Law of Karma created?

A. The Law of Karma is a means of balancing cause and effect within the centers of consciousness and thereby the portions of the Deity.

Q. But who was it created by?

A. The Universal All. The God. The Supreme Consciousness—the old man, with his long white beard to balance the goings on in the world below, created the Law of Karma, so that each cause would have its effect.

There was one reading that addressed the "problem" of peace on Earth.

Q. Do you see a time when the Earth will be at peace?

A. In the terminology, the definition 100% peace in the whole world, no. It is not the nature of Man to be at peace. This would thwart the purpose of the world. If it were complete peace, nothing would be happening. This would no longer be a place to work out that kind of conflict. For so long as there is greed, and those with greed as a motivator, and those who have and those who have not, there is going to be conflict, of some kind, in some place.

This is, indeed, a sobering statement. It paints our fifth plane home, here on Earth, as a perpetual crisis clinic, a place where peace and quiet will never reign. It appears to be much like a rock tumbler, where all the souls with rugged aggressiveness, pointed heads, jabbing elbows, and sharp tongues can abrasively wear down their protuberances against each other until they can get along together. And when they finally get their act together, maybe they can move on to the 6th plane.

But is the 6th plane all sweetness and light? Or could it be a more refined style of conflict? Maybe they just play bridge, and call the director when someone pulls a nasty trick like reneging. Seriously, it sounds as though conflict is the main educational tool used in each soul's long journey to perfection and return to God. And maybe, here on Earth, success is having arguments instead of Armageddons. And remember, there can be a lot of good experiences and encounters amid the conflicts. Now, for your daily truism—peace is so difficult to achieve because it takes 100% (or even more!) of all the souls involved to achieve it, while a minority of only one can cause conflict.

Now, back to the basic question—why are we humans here on Earth? What is our reason for being? Let us look at some possibilities.

1. DUST TO DUST. We are an advanced animal but we are born, we live, and we die, and that is that; there isn't any more. People of this persuasion usually think their only immortality might be the children they conceive and rear. Thus, procreation and survival are our prime reasons for being here. These people are usually extreme realists—if they can't sense it, it isn't there. You would be surprised, however, how many professed Christians really believe this, but are covering all bets by attending church. Remember, they are realists.

It must be admitted that there really is a possibility that there is no Supreme Being and we are simply the result of a bunch of atoms thrown together and nothing remains of us after death but a decaying body. It could be that the records Cayce and Mark quoted are figments of their imagination, or even worse, data being fed to us by some Nefilim-like advanced beings trying to control us thru kingship. It is possible that the tangible "gods" of the Old Testament, the Nefilim, became the remote monotheistic "God" of the New Testament after the Nefilim reduce their presence, thru kingship, and finally faded away altogether. Without tangible supermen to work for, the priesthood may have invented a SUPERBEING, who they represented, naturally, so they could replace the departed Nefilim as rulers. It is a possibility.

But there seems to be too much evidence to the contrary to believe there is no soul; that the body and brain are the total being and nothing from that one body survives after death. Too many people, on the borderline between life and death, have glimpsed something beyond our world. Too many people have vivid recollections of living in bygone days. And with Cayce and Mark, there is too much evidence of ties to other lifetimes.

2.   THE CHRISTIAN APPROACH. Only one lifetime, and then eternity in either Heaven or Hell. In a previous chapter, reference was made to an effort, in the 4th century A.D., by the Roman Emperor Constantine, to alter the Bible by removing most of the references to reincarnation. In satirical fashion, we described the purpose of the meeting. We will repeat it now:

"The object of the meeting was to revise the manual to strengthen the sales pitch. They hit on a brilliant idea—use the fear factor. 'You have got to get it all together in this lifetime because this is it! After this lifetime, you will spend Eternity either burning in Hell or basking in Heaven, and only us teachers have the smarts to interpret the manual and make sure you get into Heaven—only one lifetime, so depend on us!"

This is a much stronger approach than can be made for reincarnation. There, you can tell that religious leader trying to enroll you that you will just plug along on your own, because if you don't make it in this lifetime, there are lots more to go.

The gnashing of teeth out there is audible all the way to the author's desk when mention is made of the Bible as a manual for a sales pitch. Well, isn't it? It is not meant in strictly derogatory sense, but whether the Pope or Jimmy Bakker use it, they are trying to "sell" you on their interpretation of it. Maybe the best use it can be put to is for *you* to read it and interpret it *yourself.* Although revised for sales purposes, it still contains much truth and wisdom.

We have looked at various approaches to describe the How

and Why a soul functions in the big universal picture, but as we travel farther away from concrete data, we must rely less and less on facts. Let us face it; there are very few facts on the soul and spirit—it is mostly conjecture. Much of it must be built on faith.

Faith. That is a good word. Let's see what Webster has to say about faith. The first definition is a general one. Belief or trust in something or someone. The second is theological. Belief in a religious concept, as in Jesus Christ as the Son of God. The third is an intriguing one, and one we feel is closest to the truth; firm belief in something for which there is no proof.

Now, most religions stress faith very strongly. You've got to have faith, and lots of it. This is required because bad things happen to individuals in spite of right living, right thoughts, and right prayers. To a devout Christian, who has a daughter dying of cancer, a son dying of Aids, and a wife in the advanced stages of Alzheimers, the clergy can only admonish him to sin less, pray more, and have greater faith, and finally shake their heads and sigh, "The Lord moves in mysterious ways."

Faith is stressed by religious groups because, in most cases, they don't know what is causing good things or bad things to happen to a particular person any more than that person does. But by blaming any bad thing on a person's lack of faith, they retain a certain amount of power or control over that person's life. So when religion is mentioned, that is often what we are talking about—power and control. When one person tries to learn about God, or walk with God, that is spirituality. When two or more people seek God, that is religion. And the dominant of the two or more persons involved, if their motives are analyzed, will many times find power to be the prime factor. They will, of course, refuse to admit this even to themselves, but it is true in many cases.

So faith, or rather a lack of it, is frequently used by the clergy as an excuse when bad things happen to a parishioner, in spite of right thoughts, actions, and prayers. Remember our friend with the brain tumor? He had cried, "Why me?" He had been a pillar in his church and spiritually was one of the least sinful men the author has ever known. Yet in spite of leading an exemplary life, he was dying of cancer, and neither his doctors nor his church could help him because, rightly or wrongly, he was searching for pain and suffering in this lifetime. No amount of FAITH had changed that desire, and he had plenty of faith. Only when his subconscious became convinced that the suffering was not aiding him spiritually did the tumor go into remission.

What the author is getting around to is a statement of policy; the belief that faith is a poor substitute for facts. With that statement, a seemingly contradictory statement will be made. We must use faith, with caution, in areas beyond facts.

What this means is that we should, all of us, be striving to learn WHERE we came from, WHY we are here, and WHERE do we go from here. We should not strive to the point that we neglect everyday life, but we must learn about these three Ws in order to LIVE that everyday life with greater meaning. As was stated before, our evolutionary plane is so elementary that we cannot even contemplate absolute truth, but will do well if we stumble in that direction. But to make certain that we stumble in the right direction, each of us must develop our own concepts of truth.

Now to try to apply our newfound knowledge. To arrive at our new concepts on highly theoretical subjects, we uncover as many facts as we can, determine which direction most of the facts point, and then guess at the conclusion. Our faith in that conclusion should not be absolute—any new facts that come to our attention that SHOULD alter our conclusion, MUST alter our conclusion.

The effort to find the truth about ourselves will make us better equipped to live this lifetime with our fellow man. For those of us who have studied and believe such concepts as 'do unto others as you would have them do unto you' and 'what diminishes my fellow man, diminishes me', we are better fitted to live in these chaotic times. We look at the dust to dust, one lifetime person with no envy. We feel no envy for many Christians, cut off from searching for truth by a church that demands absolute adherence to its views and forbids such investigation. Yes, each one of us must use faith in areas beyond facts, but not by putting our faith in another faith that restricts or forbids an individual's mind from seeking truth for itself.

The most important element on Earth today is each individual soul, and the lessons it is learning by interacting with other souls. The physical Earth itself, and all the planets and animals, including the human bodies themselves, are simply the stage setting for these souls to interact with each other and, learning by experiences, to grow spiritually.

Now for a little nitpicking. When it is said that individual souls are the most important element on Earth, it is meant the driver part of the soul, not the navigator. Let's use another analogy here, making the driver a prize fighter and the navigator his trainer. In the corner, between rounds, the trainer can give the fighter all kinds of advice, but when the round, or lifetime starts, the fighter is mostly on his own; he is hitting and being hit. The trainer can yell, but the fighter, during the bout, is there to interact with the other fighter, and learn the lessons he is here to learn. His actions in the ring are the most important thing. We know the trainer, or navigator, or Godhood is vital, but the Earth and all physical things on it exist only for the education of the driver part of the soul.

Many will ask why put our faith in the spiritual evolution of each individual soul rather than the Bible or a particular religion. Because there have been too many incorrect translations and too much deliberate rewriting of the Bible by mortal men, for mortal purposes. We have seen the fallibility of the infallible Pope, as in the Spanish Inquisition and the current policy against any birth control on this crowded planet. The main reasons for choosing individual souls as the most important element on Earth is the track record of their advocates.

Instead of wringing their hands and crying that the Lord moves in mysterious ways, Cayce and Mark would point back to a Karma generated in a previous lifetime as the cause for seemingly implausible things happening to people in this lifetime. Mark's reading depicted the author and his wife as voyageurs in Canada in the last lifetime, which explains why the author proposed while seated in a kayak; we had lived much of our past lifetime in canoes.

We are here on Earth to grow spiritually and eventually return to God.

GOD

You are right! The really important chapter was saved until almost the last. Who, or what, is God? What is our relationship with God? Does God run the Universe, and if so, how?

Remember the technique used in the last chapter for dealing with very theoretical subjects. Weight all the facts, develop the direction the facts are leading, and then take an educated guess at an answer. This topic is so far beyond facts that it might do just as well to take out the old dart board and have a bit of a go at it. But all of us have opinions on just about every subject. Even if you have heard only one comment on a subject, you automatically analyze the character of whoever commented on it, or what media brought it to you. So we will weigh all the facts, arrive at a direction, and then make our longest cast, into the unknown, that has yet been made.

As one punster once said, Darwin and evolution are not subjects with which you want to monkey. The present era might well be called the Darwinian Age, so great has been the influence of this 19th century biologist. After his two years of observations while on board the exploration ship H.M.S. Beagle, Charles Darwin returned to England and lived in seclusion, writing and constantly revising his theories and conclusions.

Having seen many strange species of animals in South America, and particularly on the isolated Galapagos Islands, he developed his theory in which the strongest and fittest of a species would survive over weaker members of their own or a similar competing species. Darwin believed that changes occurred thru chance mutation of genes and if the change was superior to the original, the mutant would survive and in time drive out the older form. Thus the giraffes, who by some freak mutation developed a long neck enabling them to reach the leaves at the tops of the trees, would survive, multiply, and replace their shorter necked predecessors. This is diametrically opposite to the rejected theory of acquired characteristics, advanced by Lamarck in the 18th century, which contended that the giraffe was rewarded with a long neck by constantly stretching, over centuries of time, for those juicy leaves on the upper branches of trees.

In addition to the survival of the fittest, Darwin shocked the world by saying that man, monkeys, and apes developed from the same ancestral tree. Immediately, he was assailed from every pulpit. Gradually science prevailed and the Scopes trial of 1920 was the last serious attack on Darwin's theory.

Our old friend, Immanuel Velikovsky, in *Earth in Upheaval*, makes some interesting observations about Darwin's theory. Velikovsky points out that we have witnessed the second half of survival of the fittest, with the extermination of many species, such as the Tasmanian natives, south of Australia, by the white man, and the passing of the Neanderthal with the advent of Cro-Magnon Man. But we have yet to see the introduction of a new species, by mutation or otherwise, that can reproduce itself.

Formerly, the Earth abounded with many different species of the same family of animals. Excavations in the Siwallic Hills of India revealed hundreds of extinct species, including almost 30 different species of elephants, where we have but two on the entire Earth today. And in historical times, many animals have become extinct—the giant Goa bird of India and our own passenger pigeon come to mind. Yet no new species have developed.

Velikovsky surmises that evolution occurs all right—but not as pictured by Darwin. Velikovsky calls it "instantaneous evolution", caused by either cosmic, X-ray, or nuclear rays, occurring when other worlds pass close to the Earth. He cites the experiments of T.H. Morgan with drosophila, the vinegar fly. When exposed to varying degrees of X-ray, too much would kill them but lesser amounts would cause the immediate offspring to be a weird mixture. Some would be without wings, others with four legs, and others without eyes. And extreme temperatures have also shown the ability to jumble the genes and cause mutations. But in all of these cases, the changes do not carry beyond the first generation. Velikovsky believed the conditions most favorable for mutations occur during the time of cataclysms; cosmic rays, extremes in temperature, nuclear radiation, and a gigantic electrical discharge.

It is quite an idea. And other factors would assist the mutants. Our crowded world of today does not tolerate a radical new offshoot of any kind—make it conform or kill it seems to be the rule. Yet in the wake of a cataclysm, the few chance survivors, who had chosen just the right cave in which to hide, would emerge after the worst of the volcanic dust, meteor showers, lava flows, tidal waves, and extremes of temperature, into a new world. Like other handfuls of animal types and their mates, emerging from other similar refuges over widely scattered areas, they would have been exposed to stresses on their genetic makeup that we cannot imagine. When mutations occur here, there is no vast population to kill or absorb the mutants. And because of the isolation of the survivors, the genetic pool of many may stem from the genes of just two, with the forceful accentuation of characteristics, both good and bad, that is caused by the inbreeding of the founders.

It should be understood that many species of animals flourishing before a cataclysm may be wiped out to the last member. Other species may have a few survivors, but they cannot adapt to the altered environment. Yet mutant survivors from the same family may make the adjustment, survive, and multiply.

The survival of the fittest, as depicted by Darwin, does not always appear to apply. The now extinct woolly mammoth was better adapted to survive than either of our two present day elephant species. And the saber-toothed tiger would have made short work of our present day tiger. Even Darwin expressed concern of the extinction of many superior types. When viewed in the light of a cataclysmic world, accidentally to be at the right refuge at the right time counted far more than superior traits. Some insist it was still the fittest that survived; they could run faster to caves, hold their breath longer, or make better preparations. Nevertheless, all of the fittest of a great river delta city would have perished while a shepherd couple, high in the hills, might survive. So the key word "chance" still seems to dominate the end of a world age.

Another odd feature of survival can be seen in the extinction of the passenger pigeon. This prolific bird literally darkened the sky for hours at a time as they moved to new feeding rounds in the mid-western United States of the mid 1800s. So numerous and such a nuisance were they that every means were taken to get rid of them. They were dynamited, burned, and shot until their numbers dwindled from billions to mere millions. Then, however, they were unable to adapt to flights of only hundreds of thousands, and simply dwindled away—the last passenger pigeon died in 1920. They had to exist on a gigantic scale, or not at all.

Velikovsky cited another side of survival in an odd adaptation of the Mongoloid race. A body opening, allowing oxygen to reach the fetus, is larger in this race than in any other. This has no effect in our world today—unless a non-Mongoloid woman lives above the 15,000 foot level on a mountain; then the fetus will not get enough oxygen and will die. If a cataclysm caused our atmosphere to thin, it might be the answer to a question future anthropolgists might scratch their heads about—why did all of the other races except the Mongoloid vanish? Was it something this simple that caused the Neanderthal to disappear and our Cro-Magnon to survive?

Velikovsky's idea of instantaneous evolution sounded so logical that Mark was asked to do a reading on the subject. The answers were negative.

"How does evolution occur? In other words, is it chance mutations over a long period of time?"

"No"

"Is it exposure of a few survivors of a cataclysm to radiation, heat, cold, X-ray, etc?"

"Evolution is an orderly process, much as building a wall of brick is done one brick at a time. Radiation, mutation, abnormal methods are of no benefit to the species and as a result are not carried beyond the immediate generation."

"Is the pattern established for evolution actually established prior to its taking place? Is this a master plan?"

"Yes."

"In an orderly fashion?"

"Yes."

"Preordained—could you say?"

"Preordained—in the terminology of the seeker, yes."

Well, here we are on the proverbial horns of a dilemma. It appeared that Velikovsky had come up with a logical answer as to why we had seen no new species to replace the hundreds that had become extinct in historical times—all it would take would be another cataclysm to create more species. But a different source, Mark's readings, say evolution is a planned program, and not generated by a wild cataclysmic event.

Now, the author thought most data appeared to support

Velikovsky very strongly. But it would not be wise to repeat the actions of some, and sweep contrary opinions under the rug. Let us examine Mark's readings in regard to Velikovsky.

The readings supported Velikovsky on cataclysms in historical times, in sudden elevations of the Andes, and Mankind being reduced to scattered handfuls in the historical past. But they were adamant that there was purpose and intelligence over every world created. A direct quote of some of Mark's readings will give a glimpse of the possibility of an organized Universe.

"How does the Solar System operate?"

"Solar systems operate each with the Planetary Deities in conjunction with the Solar Deities in a geometric pattern, in accordance with natural laws."

"Who are the Planetary and Solar Deities which were mentioned?"

"The Planetary Deities are the deities who assume the responsibility for the creation, and therefore the location, indicated in the Divine Mind, of the planets. These, the planets, to support the creation of the Logos—the Cherbim and the Serifim. The Solar Deities are the directing and energizing deities who sacrifice their energies to bring forth the lesser deities."

"How does life develop on a new planet?"

"In accordance with the visualization in the Divine Mind and the directions to the Cherubim and Serifim, who set out to create what was visualized."

"Is it true that normally life is generated on planets but souls are created and move from planet to planet?"

"Souls are not moved from planet to planet but are created in the planetary environment for that specific planetary environment. The Spiritual Essences move from chain to chain—the Spiritual Essences only."

Now we really have a bunch of possibilities. God creating the stars and the sky and the plants and animals and Man, *OR* the Universe is just there; atoms strike each other and speed off in new directions, combining thru trial and error with other atoms and create new forms, *OR* more complex and higher developed forms come about by chance mutation, with the superior mutants replacing the parent stock, *OR* the Earth was colonized by beings from other worlds, *OR* beings from other worlds who colonized Earth created Man to work for them, but

Man ended up taking over the Earth after the alien beings moved on, *OR* God, and/or the Divine Mind, visualizes a new Solar System and lesser Deities set about to create what was visualized, and all change is controlled by the Divine Mind, acting thru lesser Deities.

What a spread of possibilities! All but the last item have been discussed, so a look will be taken at just how it might operate. Just suppose—the Universe *WAS* envisioned by the Divine Mind and built by lesser Deities creating what had been visualized. This includes not only the creation, but the revisions necessary as conditions and requirements change.

A big question would be just how these revisions are accomplished. As an example, what if the Head Umpire looked down on Planet Earth towards the end of this critical 20th century and decides that things are going to hell in a hand basket and he must shake things up a bit down there by either (1) getting word to the heads of state to shape up or else or, (2) lining up a bunch of planets in a row to make a little cataclysm. (Velikovsky may be right, after all, in that the *planned* evolutionary changes may be done during cataclysmic times, by the Deities, to give the new mutants a better chance to survive.) Or if he thought they were doing all right and might make it thru to the Aquarian Age after all, how could he lessen the impact of all those end-of-an-age bad things that always seem to happen?

How would those lesser Deities operate, if they existed? Would it be directly, by pushing a comet close to the Earth? Or would it be by sending a knowing emissary, with all the straight scoop, to the leaders of tribes or nations? Could it even be planting the seed of an idea in the mind of an unknowing being? Problems, right?

Since one main source of information on these deities are the records read by Cayce and Mark, these records had better be examined. As stated earlier, they are the records of every thought and action of every soul who has ever incarnated on Earth. Access to these records can be learned by people with spiritual awareness, after developing the self confidence of their subconsciousness. A teacher is almost a necessity (Mark's teacher did not have one, but a more grueling experience you cannot imagine). When a person learns to gain access to the records, a file keeper digs into the stacks and comes up with the information sought, whether it is a fluoroscopic picture of the body, words on a blue board, or short recap movies of critical karmic events.

There are several factors which could possibly influence the readings. (1.) The records themselves. (2.) The file keeper. (3.) The reader of the records. (4.) The interrogator. (5.) The seeker.

Now, it appears that the records themselves are just THERE, and are factual—those things really happened. Knowing that prophecies and things not related to ones spiritual growth can be in error, the readings on vital data appear to be convincing and consistent with other readings and other means of proof. And now the author will use a term repugnant to most scientists; when the author heard a reading of his past lives and karmic connections, he knew, intuitively, right in his gut, that it was true. (2.) The file keeper evidently has a lot of discretionary power. He can refuse to reveal karmic information if it would lessen the freedom of choice of the ones who must work out the Karma in the current lifetime. After all, isn't that why they are here; to learn by making their own decisions?

The file on each soul must be a rather large one. Once, when a seeker failed to specify that he wanted his three prime Karmas, the file keeper said he had 428 Karmas in hand. (3.) The conscious mind of the reader can have an influence on the readings. Occasionally, on topics dear to the heart of the reader, Mark will stop, say that the conscious mind intrudes, and rephrase a position. (4.) The interrogator can have an impact on the readings. He or she is the anchor and lifeline the reader must have when he is traveling to, examining, and returning from the records. Mark has done no readings since his wife, who did the interrogating, died several years ago. (5.) The seeker can influence by seeking but not seeking; by wanting to know but being afraid to find out. Many times the seeker will skirt around vital questions, but the readings will often address these problems areas, anyway.

Now for some random conclusions. It appears that the Akashic and Cosmic Records are just *there*, are factual, and are sitting there for anyone with the ability to read them. There are many people who could learn to read them, as Mark did in just a few weeks, but there are also many more like the author, whose conscious mind so dominates the subconscious mind that it would be a real chore to learn.

There seems to be a possibility, at least to the author, that each person's Godhood, or Divine Essence, is the file keeper. Remember that as the human body is the vehicle for the soul, the soul is the vehicle, in this planetary system, for the Divine Essence, or Godhood. This Godhood knows the requirements for the spiritual growth of the soul in its custody down to a tee. It knows when to hold back information that would be detrimental for the soul's spiritual development. It may make vital decisions concerning the soul's development after consulting with other advanced beings or deities, but it seems as though it makes most of the vital decisions, such as when to incarnate next in order to work out which Karma and with whom.

There is also a possibility that the conscious mind of the reader of the records does intrude to some small extend into the readings, but not enough to distort the intended message. Mark is also a Conservative, and may be a little more derisive about "do-gooders" in readings than necessary, but the story is consistent from reader to reader. The most important target for Liberals, intent on saving souls, should be—themselves! Get your own house in order before trying to save others. Spiritual growth occurs when the driver makes a correct moral decision on his own. Outside help should be limited; a good way is to show by example. Outside help, permanent and crutching, which lessens the driver's resolve to make his own decisions, is detrimental. This is very emphatic in the readings (there can be one other factor—the author. By his choice of items to quote from the readings, he can also influence, even though he tries to keep it as objective as possible).

Now for an idea about control on Planet Earth. We have started that periodic cataclysms are a probability here. If you had been surveying for a world on which to establish a colony, would you choose Earth? Maybe it *is* a penal colony, and the only control is containment; keeping those rambunctious characters from contaminating the surrounding space and nearby civilizations. And maybe the little Divine Essence, hidden in each soul of each human on Earth, is the prime control for that being. But you must remember that the control is almost non-existent during the actual incarnation. That poor little Divine Essence is more like a cowboy trying to stay on the back of Brahma Bull in a rodeo—he is just along for the ride. But in between incarnations, this Godhood determines what Karma will be worked, what other souls will be involved, and when they will incarnate in the next lifetime.

A confession will be made right now. Much of this chapter has been written right off the top of the head, while waiting for Divine Inspiration. This idea of the Divine Essence doing the major part of the shepherding of its soul, coming like a bolt from the blue, does seem to have a lot of merit.

This point, right here, was to have been just about the end of this chapter. A few snappy windup sentences and you would be turning to the next chapter. But there was a feeling that something was missing. The subject is Love and until about one hour ago, there were no coherent thoughts on it. But while the author was lying in bed, at 6:30 A.M., something came thru.

Being sort of a rugged individualist, the author has shied away from lending a helping hand, if that hand might thwart (that word from a reading is a good one) the aided person's attempt to accomplish something by his or her own effort. It is like the reaction of many to one of Nelson Decker's little pamphlets, entitled "Be Positively Selfish." His premise is that we should get our own act together before charging out to save everybody else. Good sense, but the term selfish sticks in a person's craw.

And the last little discovery that the role of our Godhood, here on Earth, might be a major, almost exclusive, part of our soul's guidance and assessment, fits in with a different slant on the term love. And it is spelled L-O-V-E, not L-U-S-T. We are speaking of brotherly or sisterly love.

In earlier chapters, we expressed a little cynicism in the Biblical use of the words meek and humble and, by association, the term love as a means of the clergy to gain control over the laity of any church. We think meek and humble were added when the Bible was revised to strengthen the sales pitch but we think the original version probably put even greater emphasis on love. Love is the key—not meek and humble.

Much metaphysical material indicates that we, as individual souls, progress upward as we grow spiritually. Today, this individual soul is in the Earth plane, and by the output of a lot of good effort over many, many lifetimes, will leave all the rest of the 5th plane souls and go on to the 6th plane on some other world, where it will join other 6th plane souls, struggling with other kinds of conflict.

But metaphysics is not monolithic. A small minority think we stay here on Earth until a majority of us reach a certain level of spiritual growth, at which time we *all* go to the 6th plane—like a fifth grade class graduating to the 6th grade. But with one very big difference. The amount of the time spent in this 5th plane is determined by the spiritual growth of the average soul. At a certain average SAT score, we all move up, but it might take a zillion years for one bunch but two zillion for the next bunch.

You ask how does love enter into all of this? Right here—you may be positively selfish, and make great spiritual strides, but you must remember that there exists a possibility that you will not leave this plane until *everyone* grows spiritually, so we better give a compassionate, and constructive helping hand whenever possible. WE ARE *ONE* WITH EVERY OTHER SOUL ON EARTH, SO WHAT DIMINISHES THEM, DIMINISHES US.

It is like one person being a hand of a body and another person being the foot of the same body. Say that you, as the foot, are doing well and feeling fine, but that fella over there, the hand, is so crippled with arthritis that he can't hold a shovel anymore and because of that fact, the whole body can't continue it's job of ditch digging to put food on the table. Your feeling for him can't be a cool clinical sympathy—*HE IS A PART OF YOU!*, and what ails him, ails you. It can not be stressed too heavily that we are one with every soul on Earth—when Mankind as a whole suffers, each one of us suffers.

The dictionary doesn't make much distinction between sympathy and compassion, but we think compassion comes closer to what we should feel for our fellow being. "Sympathetic consciousness of others distress together with a desire to help them alleviate it," to which we add the word "themselves."

So have compassion for those who are not advancing spiritually, but make it a constructive compassion, as their "non growth" may have a direct impact on you—it may lengthen your own stay on this 5th plane. This compassion should not be a sly, calculated compassion, as mentioned earlier of a person going to church to cover all bets, just in case there is a heaven. It must be "heartfelt, or more aptly, soulfelt."

The author has been procrastinating on one topic until he is finally running out of both time and space. The topic is Jesus Christ. You can talk all you want about tilting and jousting with windmills, but when you discuss objectively the relationship of Jesus Christ with GOD, you *know* you will be treading on many toes. But that is the whole purpose of this book—to show the reader that there should never be any restraints put on a person's striving for the TRUTH. If what the author puts down here in his effort to "stumble towards the truth" is not acceptable to the reader, all well and good—at least he or she has been exposed to a different concept.

Remember when we spoke of Hoyle stating that if only one chance in one million existed that a planet within range of our current radio telescopes could support human life, there would be one million chances. Then we learned that the range of our radio telescopes was very limited, and other parts of the Universe very likely exist that are contracting while our local area appears to be expanding. So it could well be that there are probably BILLIONS of planets in the Universe that could support life. It is becoming more and more difficult for the author to believe that Earth is the only world in the entire Universe with intelligent(?) life. The chances are more likely that there are millions or even billions of worlds supporting life, with some of the life being quantum leaps more advanced than Homo Sapiens on planet Earth.

Now when the Bible speaks of Jesus of Nazareth being the Son of God, the author has no quarrel with that concept—because he believes that *every* soul is the Son (or Daughter) of God. Each one of us was sent out originally from God to interact with other souls, and from this interaction over long periods of time, to grow spiritually and finally return to God. The argument the author has with the Bible is the position of Jesus of Nazareth in the overall scheme of things. The Bible states that Jesus Christ was the personification of GOD, the Right Hand of GOD, and was the only such personification around, and HE incarnated here on Earth to teach Mankind the "True Path." The author's problem is that if this single monothestic figure is going to incarnate on all of the millions or billions of planets with lifeforms, HE really has HIS work cut out for HIM. The author will accept the fact that Jesus of Nazareth was an Ascended

Master and had, according to Cayce, incarnated on this Earth before as, if our memory is correct, Melchizedek and Enoch. He may well be the most influential Ascended Master who ever trod this planet; but he is just one of many Ascended Masters, all of whom are doing their job.

The author is not trying to belittle the role of Jesus; he thinks the New Testament expanded and glorified the role, in order to awe the readers with the exalted position of the Prophet of Nazareth, and to bring new members into this new church.

One problem biblical scholars have wrestled with for some time is trying to figure out just what makes up the Trinity. The Father, the Son, and the Holy Ghost; exactly who are they? While most think of definitions on a macrocosm scale, the author thinks the answer could be down to the microcosm. Might the Trinity be referring to the occupants of each soul incarnated on this Earth? Could the father be the Divine Essence (the Godhood), and the Son be the driver (the conscious mind), and the Holy Ghost be the CB operator (the subconscious mind)?

Now for another confession; so much of this is so far beyond facts that the author doesn't know what he is talking about! Oh, heads are nodding out there!. But that is what this chapter, in fact the whole book, is all about; getting the reader to think beyond the Soaps, the Pennant Race, and the Workplace. If you are starting to say, "He must be wrong on this point—I think it is this way," it is a big step in the right direction. At least the mental juices are starting to flow.

Now for a summation. There seems to be Intelligence, Purpose, and a Master Plan for the Universe. Just how this plan is carried out is uncertain. One possibility appears to be the idea of "The Big Guys" doing it, the Divine Mind and the Deities doing the world-moving events, though it could be that beings, either knowingly or unknowingly, may do much of the nuts and bolts work. At a local world level, there may be a consensus of opinion of all the centers of consciousness on that world, a vote if you like, for the course of action needed on that planet. For example, if it is the end of one age and the start of another, as we are about to start the Aquarian Age on Earth, we think these local Godhoods can vote on the severity of the transition, and a majority vote of all the Godhoods here on Earth one way or the other way may carry a lot of weight "UPSTAIRS." If they decide to wipe the slate almost clean, and start anew with scattered handfuls, they can do it (this upcoming transition, in the next two decades, will be rough, the author thinks, but not down to scattered handfuls). Whether they can do it themselves, collectively, or have to call in a Cherubim or two, is unknown. But each Godhood appears to have the main responsibility for the guidance of the soul in his keeping to the best learning sequence in resolving its Karma, and there may be a remote possibility that we graduate to the next plane en mass.

For those of you who want an anthropomorphic (humanlike) God, you will probably be disappointed. "God" seems to be in every atom of the universe. As to the "high muckimucks", the guy or guys who make the big decisions, regardless of what kind of form it or they take, or even whether it or they are visible or invisible to us, it just might be a committee, like a Board of Directors, say the 12 highest evolved beings in the whole shebang. They might meet every Thursday, from 9 till 5. Thursday was chosen because, you know how it is—Monday is for the laundry, bowling league is on Tuesday, and of course, Wednesday is *always* reserved for golf—!

The name of this chapter brings to mind a joke about a rectal surgeon and a psychiatrist who happened to share a common waiting room. They hired a painter to stencil their names and titles on the door from the hallway into the waiting room, but he complained that there was not enough room for both the names and the titles on the small window of the door. They told him to shorten the titles and went back to work.

Later, the painter called them out to see what he had done. They took one look, shook their heads, and turned to go back to work. Under the names the painter had stenciled "rears and queers." One of them said as they left, "Try again."

Once again the painter called them out for approval, and this time they deliberated some time before shaking their heads. They finally told the painter he was getting close and to try again. The sign read "nuts and butts."

When the two doctors were summoned again, they took one look, smiled, and nodded their heads. You guessed it! The sign under the names read "odds and ends."

This chapter will be the trivia corner, mentioning things too short for a chapter, winding up loose ends, and covering overlooked items.

1.   CONSERVATIVES VS. LIBERALS. Just in case the reader hasn't tumbled to the fact, the author is an unabashed Conservative. Some will say it is oxymoronic (extreme opposites). How can anyone stressing that each human's main reason for being on this Earth is spiritual growth, be one of those money-grubbing Conservatives? You know the type; the skinflints always trying to cut welfare payments and entitlements that the bleeding heart Liberals are always trying to increase. Isn't this speaking with forked tongue?

Let us take one look at what the readings say about helping your fellow man. First of all, great skepticism was leveled at most efforts of what the readings literally termed "do-gooders" to assist other people (remember that Mark remembers almost nothing of what he says while in the trance). Most assistance, if it merely extends and perpetuates a negative situation, such as a poverty level life-style, is considered detrimental. Remember that in the readings, there is no good or bad. This is not immoral; this is simply stating that ideas of good and bad vary from age to age. Human sacrifices in South America and witch hunting in Salem were considered "good" at one time. Filling an empty stomach but requiring no effort on the part of that person is not necessarily beneficial. An empty stomach can be a great motivating force. The early development of the United States was a history of the motivating force of hunger, or at least of its possibility.

The United States today is divided into two groups of people. One is mainstream America—those who work for a living, pay taxes, put food on their table by the sweat of their brow, or have done so and are now retired. Another group, a growing minority, are doing no work, but are also living on the sweat of the brow of mainstream America (there is also a growing grey area group of those who work, but pay no taxes). The more money Congress puts into a safety net they have erected under our free enterprise system, the greater number of people opt to leave mainstream America, stop working and/or paying taxes, and ride along with the flow. Human nature (animal nature?) has not yet evolved to the point where most average citizens will shake their heads and say, "No—even if I could get a fair amount of money the rest of my life by not working, I would still rather work."

A case in point is AFDC (Aid for Families of Dependent Children). Some of you out there may think the SKI-BUM bit in the chapter on Politics was a little too blunt. Possibly, but an article in a newspaper last year told of a 24 year old woman with eight children, who received $950 a month in welfare and food stamps, plus "several hundred dollars a month in rental assistance." No mention was made of the fathers of the children. But this woman, starting in her mid teens, found that the best paying job she could find was raising her illegitimate children. That our Congress would fund this program to the point of literally (Liberally?) breeding millions more like her, with no incentive to change the condition, is a tragedy. The impact on lower income families, particularly black families, has been devastating. As an example, in 1960, 78% of black families had two parents in the household; 20% had a woman only. By 1988, only 39% of black households have two parents; 60% are headed by a woman only. Another statistic may be the major cause of this trend—from 1960 to 1988, the amount of money spent annually on AFDC increased over 160 times, to over $16,000,000,000.

Statistics tell us that single parent families are not as good as two parent families. A transient father figure is not enough. Rather than "crutching the cripples" with massive day care for single parent families, the thrust should be to change the welfare laws to encourage two parent families. A one parent family is like a one legged human—laboring under a handicap. The typical day care center is a poor substitute for a two parent family. And even worse is the cyclic nature of these single parent families. The majority of children born in the city of Chicago are born out of wedlock, and it can be assumed that the other metropolitan cities have similar figures. Think of the stifling intellectual atmosphere where the only family head has had little or no employment, and is usually a high school dropout. No wonder when the children from these families enter school, to them it is like an alien world and they often drop out, just as the mother had done.

Compassion should be felt for those welfare children; they are simply the result of a Congress too busy throwing money at a problem to see the harm they are enlarging and perpetuating. Those people *must* be dragged into main stream America and their incentive to stay on AFDC be reduced.

2.   GUNS. The right to bear arms is given by the Bill of Rights in our Constitution, but do you really think our founding fathers would approve of an AK-47 over every fireplace. Back in the 1950s, larger caliber semi-automatic weapons that were capable of being converted to fully automatic fire were outlawed. In recent years, the ruling has been relaxed to the point where we are awash in Russian, Chinese, and Israeli automatic weapons. This is a big mistake; during a grace period, they should all be turned in and after that, a stiff minimum sentence given to anyone with one in their possession.

3.   QUALITY OF LIFE. The author and his family feel strongly about the quality of life around us, in the places where we live. We want to live in a town of less than 50,000 population that is smog-free. That does not mean a suburb of a smoky city. As an example, our "down" home in Arizona, where we reside almost six months of the year, is in an RV park on a lake three

miles from a town of less than 30,000, with no larger towns within 125 miles. The people are friendly and petty crime exists only for a short period when young spring-break Californians come in by the droves. We have adequate shopping and we average a concert or some presentation about once a week. We are as busy as we want to be. Speaking personally, golf 2 or 3 times a week, tennis twice a week, sailing when there is wind (I have over 12,000 miles on a little 12' cat), retrieving golf balls from the lake near a golf course when there is no wind, and a weekly trip to the casinos at Laughlin.

The better half, besides golf at least once a week, runs the bridge group at the park, and manages to play about 6 days a week. We eat out at good, inexpensive restaurants about 3 times a week. Financially, our friends range from just above Social Security level to wealthy; the amount of money a couple has above the $250 a month for their space in the park and for food is not very important. It is a healthy, low key, do-what-you-want-to-do environment. A fella can even write a book in his spare time, or ride a motorcycle a 1000 miles a winter in the sparse and slow-paced traffic.

Our "up" town home overlooks Puget Sound seven miles from a 20,000 population town about 35 miles from Seattle. Though probably too low keyed and informal for most, we thoroughly enjoy our quality of life.

4.   ABORTION. Because of the author's belief in both reincarnation and his conservative views, you can be sure there was some real study on the abortion issue. First a look at the reincarnationist's view. The majority feel that the soul enters the baby anywhere from a few days prior to birth to a few hours after birth. The soul has been around the mother and father for some time, evaluating the parents thoughts and actions before making the final decision to enter. It is studying a very complex matrix at this time. It is looking at this particular baby being born at this particular time because it will grow up and meet another soul with which there is a major karma to be worked. If the fetus is aborted, the soul must look for another body, possibly in another lifetime, in which to work out this particular karma. It may, instead, choose another karma to work out in this lifetime, or even wait till later to incarnate.

So how does abortion effect all of this? It is the author's

opinion that an unwanted baby is a worse thing than an aborted fetus. There are certainly enough babies being born today without adding unwanted ones. If the only impact of an abortion is the removal of one vehicle as an entry into this tim period, so be it; there are millions more. Neither the Catholic Church nor the Republican Party should be dabbling in this affair; it is a matter for the two creators of life to decide, with the mother having the major say.

5. PROPHECY. When it comes to prophecies, their track records should be considered. One that has stood up very well was printed in a magazine such as Sage or True back about 1961 or 1962. According to the article, about 50 years ago, a blind man named McDermitt gave a written interpretation of the Kali Yuga World Cycles to a Nora Forest in Pittsburgh. This was a Cabalistic cycle divided into seven year periods extending from 1912 to the year 2010. The last period, from 2003 to 2010, is supposed to be the beginning of a thousand years of peace. McDermitt had received the antique record from an Indian national sometime after World War I. Using a good deal of astrology, it had accurately predicted the two World Wars, The Depression, the Cold War (the war that was not a war), The first Catholic president, and Pope John XXIII (the flower of flowers, and the apex of the Catholic Church).

But the most eye-catching statements were two statements in the 1989-1996 time period; "Optimism and belief in goodness and peace may lead to a blindness about troublesome things people do not want to see or believe. During the second half of this cycle comes the Third Woe, with world-wide calamities." The First and Second World Wars were called the first and second "woes."

This doesn't mean that everyone should run out and built a bomb shelter, or alter their plans of living each day to the fullest. It is just a prophecy, so the best approach is continue to live one day at a time, thanking God for giving us this lifetime in which to live. What will be, will be (admittedly easy for a 65 year old to say).

6. SENIOR CITIZENS. Much has been written about the poor starving senior citizens, but hasn't the pendulum swung a little too far? The income of the 65-74 age group is exceeded only the 45-54 group. To the seniors cry that they have paid

their dues, compare what they pay into Social Security with what our children are paying now. Even when you have factored out inflation, our kids are paying much more than we did. In AARP (the American Association of Retired People), the oldsters have one of the most powerful lobbies in the nation. They sponsor laws favorable for elderly entitlements and the right to work as long as they want. Please understand that we are not advocating a cup of hemlock, as they gave to all people 70 years old long ago on the island of Kea in Greece. But it doesn't seem fair for everyone else to foot the bill for free ski lift tickets (which we have used—animal nature, right?), Golden Passports, etc. A 10% discount would be fair.

The United States is at its best when it treats everyone equally. It is at its worst when it caters to every whim of special interest groups, as we all scramble to get in on the giveaways of the "give-ment."

We stand in too many lines (grocery, restaurant, and movie) hearing the elderly talking of their last or next cruise, while the young parents, many times both of them working, worry about stretching their food budget. More of the entry level jobs nowadays are low paying service jobs with lower expectations than the typical heavy industry jobs of previous years. Why don't we give the kids a break—tax Social Security payments as regular income. That would be the fair way to do it.

7.   DRUGS. Drugs were not yet much of a factor when our children attended junior and senior high schools in the mid 1960s. The classes immediately following them began to have drug-related problems. We did a reading with Mark, comparing the effects of smoking a cigarette with smoking a joint of marijuana (you know, that old-fashion stuff). Readings always compare physical, mental, and spiritual effects, and the reading was rather long and tedious thru the physical and mental parts, where it rated the two as about the same degree of detriment. But when it started on the spiritual impact, there was no hesitation—the marijuana was much worse. It caused what the reading termed a devolution of spiritual development, with its continued use causing a downward spiritual spiral. And LSD was "a hundred times worse than the marijuana." This is before cocaine was the "in" thing, but it can be assumed that cocaine would fall in between the marijuana and the LSD, as to its

detrimental effect, but probably closer to the LSD.

We don't know the answer to drugs. Like Cal Coolidge, when asked how he felt about sin, replied that he "was agin it." Well, we are agin drugs. Legalizing them is certainly not the answer. We think stronger family education might be an answer, but realize that in many cases, the parents of today are a major part of the problem.

8. AIDS. The subject of AIDS has been debated and analyzed from all angles, so not much space will be used. One thing that intrigues the author is the question of whether AIDS blossomed in earlier ages as well. A curious item, when reading the Old Testament, is the "thou shalt not" list. Eat no pork was on the list. Pigs, in those bygone days, apparently was the unclean animal the Bible warned about—not the carrier of AIDS, but of other diseases.

Another forbidden item was sodomy—the Old Testament carried on at length about that abomination. Now in any primitive society, homosexual behavior was discouraged, or even forbidden, because the over-riding purpose of the largest political unit in such a society was—survival!—and homosexuality was a threat to that purpose. The Old Testament could well have had that in mind. But lurking in the background is the thought that maybe the Old Testament WAS speaking from actual experiences and Mankind had an earlier encounter with AIDS and the encounter was traumatic enough to warrant putting sodomy on the "thou shalt not" list. Although AIDS is now transmitted by needles and heterosexual contact as well as homosexual contact, the original onslaught from Africa in the current wave appears to have been by homosexual means. The Old Testament is quite a book! It may well have been right about the sons of the Nefilim mating with the daughters of Man and, on an unrelated subject, it also may have known from experience that sodomy was dangerous.

Since we seem to be skating around the edge of the topic of homosexuality, an attempt will be made to give one possible cause of that condition in some people. Understand that the author is doing this right off the top of the head; no Gallop or Roper polls, or the copy of the Encyclopedia Britannica by his elbow. In primitive societies, survival was the main drive, and anything which might hinder it was discouraged. Those animals (and man is an animal) with decided homosexual traits did not pass their genes on to future generations. As the primitive society advanced to become a civilization, survival was assured by the increasing numbers, and procreation was not the vital drive in all people that it was before.

Remember the little description of just how Dianetics words—things heard when in physical pain or painful emotion can cause engrams which can have a lifelong effect. In a primitive society, although there was a lot of pain, there were probably few engrams, because the drive for survival was simple—the male chose the best mate to produce the best child to aid in the survival of the family, or extended family. Language was simple, so that even when the reactive mind was in control, it understood the language. "Get food, watch out for the rhino," etc.

Now look at modern times. An inquisitive boy is caught fondling a neighborhood girl by the girl's father, who yells bloody murder at the boy's father, who takes his belt and his son out to the woodshed. Between the blows of the belt, you can hear the father say, "If I EVER catch you touching a girl again like you did, I'll hit you twice as hard!!!" (physical pain and certainly painful emotion). The reactive mind heard it loud and clear, from the authority figure, and he said EVER, so I can't touch a girl EVER again. If the boy can't touch girls, he must touch something else—boys!

The other side of the coin is a battered mother telling her daughter in tearful detail (painful emotion) how her husband beats her and tells the impressionable girl, who has seen her mother being beaten, never to trust men or date them. That leaves girls, right? (believing in reincarnation, the author thinks another cause of homosexuality could be the change in sex from the last lifetime to the present one. Both ideas are food for thought).

9.   BUDGET DEFICIT. 36 states have passed a law calling for a constitutional amendment to force Congress to balance the annual budget. Two more states must pass such a law before a constitutional convention can be called. This seems to be the only possible way to curb the congressional mania for deficit spending. The deficit is the No. 2 danger to the United States today (the No. 1 danger is still nuclear war). If it looked like two

more states would pass such a bill, Congress would immediately pass their own version and tell the states their version is not required. But the congressional version would be so watered down as to be useless. If that ploy failed, they would probably attempt to admit the District of Columbia as a state, thus requiring another state to pass such a law.

If two more states passed such a law, the convention could demand that starting the next year, and every year thereafter, Congress could spend not a dime more than they received in taxes. Congress would moan and groan and say they could not do it the first year, but to stretch it out over five years. That is just what they said about the Graham-Rudman Bill, and the deficit each year is as high as ever. They would have to do it NOW! Currently, they are draining away the lifeblood of this nation. We are competing against the economies of Japan, Germany, and other countries like a thoroughbred horse in a high stakes race, running with a 150 pound handicap.

Last year, including those siphoned funds from Social Security, which we will sorely need in future years, Congress spent $219,000,000,000 more than they received in taxes. This year, we had to pay $160,000,000,000 in interest on the debt, just to tread water, so to speak, and that rate is going up over $17,000,000,000 every year. Any break in the longest bull market in history will find us in dire straits and now the S & L fiasco. Move over Mexico and Brazil—make room for Uncle Sam!

10.   THINGS TO DO LIST. Everybody should have a "things to do" list of deeds to accomplish in this lifetime. This is over and above your requirements for spiritual growth. There was always such a list in our family, with Helen contributing about two thirds of the items. They can be anything; a hot air balloon ride, taking the kids (and ourselves) to Europe, sponsoring a foreign student at the university, a glider ride, writing a book, a parasail ride, a white water rafting trip, and a five month, two carryon flight bag, no hotel reservations trip to Europe for the two of us. Now on the list, a trip to Norway; our school director son and his wife are currently working there.

The list need not be only big expensive items. In our "down" home, an artist taught acrylic painting classes in our park. For $10, you were provided with paints, brushes, canvas, plus video and personal instruction. The class was fantastic! The last picture attempted by the author had been over 50 years ago, and the house had been a square with a triangle on top for a roof. Last year, six lessons resulted in 6 pictures, some of them good enough to frame. Helen was even dragged away from bridge long enough for one lesson, the result of which was good enough for framing.

So make your list. How about volunteer work? Several people in our park drive vans for senior citizen activities. Or a mental activity—Genealogy? How about a course in adult education? Or a session in an Elderhostel class, anywhere in the world? Whatever it is, write it down and hang it on the wall, so it will be staring you in the face; you will be more likely to do it.

11.   FREEDOM. The current condition of country after country in eastern Europe casting off the chains of Communism and embracing democracy has brought a feeling of euphoria to the western world. But it is a time period wrought with danger. Hardline fingers still hover over nuclear buttons. Also, people with no experience in running free institutions in a free country are taking over the administration of totalitarian countries that have been limping on the ragged edge of bare survival, economically speaking. This is almost an impossible task. And sitting in the wings watching are those who gave up the power, hoping the neophytes will fall flat on their faces. Let us hope that the major freedom these new leaders find out about is not the freedom for their people to starve. Let us hope disillusionment and chaos do not drive the people back to their former rulers.

There is going to be a universal need for the proverbial helping hand. The fine line between temporary constructive assistance by the West, like our Marshall Plan after the Second World War, and the permanent welfare approach of the U.S. Congress, merely creating greater dependency, can be the difference between freedom and chaos for these people. Grobachev reminds one of a person starting an avalanche, and then running frantically ahead of it, trying to give it direction. This is an impossible task.

To a country whose work tempo has been governed for decades by fear, the removal of that fear, with no wage incentives to work harder, will lead to economic chaos. Add to this the rising nationalism being seen in both "Mother Russia" and other republics, you have a powder keg.

On top of all else, you have the real struggle between the old conservative communists, bemoaning the break-up of their orderly and all-powerful world, and the youth and have-nots, giddy with a sip and vision of freedom.

It will be interesting to see how history rates George Bush's hands off approach, first used in China and them repeated in Lithuania. He is probably right, not allowing active U. S. opposition to be used by Grobachev as a rallying cry for the masses, used by the Soviets so often and effectively in the past. Who would have believed a few months ago that now billions of aid to the U.S.S.R. is being considered.

No crystal ball can fortell the happenings in the next decade, but isn't it an interesting time to be living, with the breath of freedom sweeping around the globe?

12. MANKIND VS. PERSONKIND. After glancing back thru this book, a shocking fact emerged. The term "man" has been used about 20 times more often than the term "person." Imagine the scowls on the faces of the NOW and ERA advocates. The author humbly apologizes, stating his only defense is these two groups were unknown during most of his lifetime and the majority of anthropology, geology, and history books use the term "man" to denote Mankind. Now, if a computer or word processor were available, it would be easy to go back thru the book and make all those corrections, but imagine laboring, with some correction tape, over a 25 year old Sears portable with sticky keys—come on, gals; have a heart!

14. (because 13 is unlucky!) EDUCATION. When the author attended school, the goal of education was excellence. Few of us came close to achieving it, but we were better students for striving towards the unattainable goal. Like Don Quixote, we dreamed the impossible dream. Today the goal of education appears to be mediocrity; don't set the goals too high or you will lose the slow learners. Also, some psychologists fear that setting the goals too high will frustrate the bottom half of the class. Well, the author's older brother graduated from college at the age of 19 as a Phi Beta Kappa, while the author had to struggle to achieve a B average, but he still did not feel frustrated. If your goal is mediocrity, few will attain it, as the lack of challenge will turn off both the top and average students and even the slow students will know they are underachieving. High standards spark

interest from all levels of students. The author's high school history teacher made history so interesting that the author took more history in college than any other subject. When that high school history teacher retired, her current senior class asked her what was the first thing she would like to do. Her reply of a trip down the Nile set a goal for that class. They contacted many of the teacher's former students—and raised enough money for her trip. Excellent teachers striving for excellence in any subject will arouse and hold interest in any classroom. Mediocrity, in both teachers and curriculum, will breed boredom.

15.   ART. Just when it looked like there were no more windmills left on the horizon for our lance, we spotted one, right over there—see the one with the sign, National Endowment of the Arts, on the side. Golly; of all the snouts that should not be in the federal trough, that is the main one. Maybe when Congress gets the deficit down to zero and has a surplus, (that day will, indeed, be the millennium) then let them spend a little on NEA. We know that saying anything against the arts is a no no—right up there like being against Mom and apple pie. But you should see what some sick minds are spending your tax dollars on in the name of "the arts." It will turn your stomach. Better no tax dollars at all if part of it is going to be spent on such filth. Worth-while art can support itself. Much of what is supported by the NEA is not supported by the average citizen. Why have NEA if its primary drive appears to be to "modernize and warp" art standards.

16.   IRAQ. Iraq swallows Kuwait and the U.N. allies dig in. What will happen now? Remember that Kali Yuga prophecy, stating World War III would start between mid 1993 and the end of 1996? Six months ago, who would have thought it might be Arabs against other Arabs and the rest of the world. If fighting starts, Iraq will certainly drag Israel into it, and thus draw many Arab recruits and even Arab countries to the Iraqi side, making it a Holy War. But this may not be the war the prophecy spoke of. The author advises keeping a sharp eye on the Soviets, for any maskirovka, or mischief. This means watching both the Soviet "mechanics" in Iraq and ALWAYS those Soviet ICBMs everywhere, as those missile forces have never been stronger and are still the greatest external threat to the U.S.

Now that we are fresh out of windmills, let's move on to the epilogue.

EPILOGUE

After glancing thru the previous chapters, it must be admitted that very diverse subjects have been analyzed—a real potpourri, if you will; and succotash, if you won't. At this point, a favorite word will be introduced; glean—to find those extra kernels from a well swept field. The entire purpose of this book has been to bring to the attention of the reader that there is much to be gleaned from fields thought to be completely harvested. It brings to mind an old joke about an Indiana corn farmer on his first visit to Florida. When asked how he liked bananas, he grimaced, "Tried one once—tasted terrible; and the cob was so mushy, I could hardly hold on to it." Apparently in some fields the experts, like our Indiana farmer, missed the crop and harvested chaff instead.

The reader may have noticed the lack of any bibliography in this little book. It was done on purpose; if you wish to find out additional information on subjects covered here, you must go to the few titles or authors mentioned and expand your reading from there. Where Sitchin, and particularly Velikovsky, use an accurate rifle on their subjects, backed up by complete bibliographies, the author uses a sawed off shotgun, spraying little known pearls of wisdom all over the place. Why? Look how these two men have been accepted. Sitchin is virtually unknown and Velikovsky, in spite of the verification of many of his theories by space probes and travelers, has been accepted by but a handful of scientists in the fields of Astronomy, Physics, Geology and History.

Everyone knows what BS stands for—Bachelor of Science (also bull droppings!). And MS is Master of Science (also *More* of *Same*). And PHD is Doctor of Philosophy (or *Piled Higher* and *Deeper*). It has been said that PHDs learn more and more about less and less until they know everything about nothing. Joking aside, it does appear that in many cases, time spent in graduate school is often used to thicken the layer of encrusted "approved facts" surrounding the student. Rejected theories become nonfacts, never to be thought of or mentioned again.

In this little book, the effort has been made to expand the minds of the readers. Think of some very heavily encrusted individual, guru in a highly specialized field, reluctantly nodding his head over some bit of this shotgun wisdom that is completely unrelated to his specialty. He might even scratch his beard and comment to himself that maybe—just maybe—some of those other wild statements might be true. And then, who knows, but maybe he might stand back a little and take a good look at some of those encrusted "approved facts" he ingested 'way back in graduate school that pertain to his own field. How do they stand up in today's world? Are they really believable now? With this subtle shotgun approach, the guru above might be reached where a frontal attack on his own special field of endeavor would simply cause him to stiffen his pride—and his defenses. Well, we can dream, can't we?

The author thinks by using the new scientific method, truth can be found in all sort of odd places. Take nothing as gospel; there are no sacrosanct theories. Einstein's theory of relativity and the "insurmountable barrier" of the speed of light require attention. Every ancient historian should be reread and if his graphic descriptions of his first hand observations, in conjunction with other historians, do not fit into our fine theories of what happened back then, we should reevaluate our fine theories.

Besides a treasure trove of history in our libraries, waiting to be gleaned, there are hundreds of thousands of Sumerian Texts, still untranslated. Think of how much we could add to our knowledge of our possible ancestors—the Nefilim.

As a start on your adventure, read Velikovsky, Sitchin, and about Cayce, and the books that stir your interest after reading those three men, this before leveling your lance at windmills of your own choice. But don't take the three men named above as gospel, either. Remember that Mark's reading on Sitchin says his version of the creation of Man is only allegorically true. But from all appearances, these three men are stumbling in the right direction and appear to be much closer to the truth than the prevailing theories. And always keep in mind that any new fact that alters your own theory, *must* be weighed and added to the matrix.

The author has been admonished by many friends to lighten his approach and be upbeat about some of the more controversial areas of this book, but it is felt that some issues cannot be sugar-coated or glossed over. Sometimes if the truth is stark and bleak, such as the long term effect of our growing federal debt, the shock of presenting it in its true light (that is the reason all those zeros were used instead of calling them billions of dollars) may get the message thru to people who refuse to even think about the gravity of the situation. But that is what we should ALL be searching for, isn't it? In all fields of endeavor, with all of our strength, we should all be searching for—THE TRUTH! If this search for the TRUTH gets into the reader's blood as strongly as it had infected the author, you will be embarking on a voyage that will occupy you for the rest of your life.

Let us end with two thoughts. The first is that one of the prime reasons we were put here on Earth, right behind spiritual growth in importance, is to learn to use that thing sitting on our shoulders that keeps our ears apart. And its use is not to be restricted to just deciding which church, professor, newscaster, or art critic we should accept as our guru, and then let them fill our heads with their opinions. The reason we were placed on this Earth is to assimilate facts, weigh and sift them, and then come up with OUR OWN ideas of the TRUTH.

The second idea is that we should face up to the probability that the actions and thoughts of each one of the human race are the most important dramas happening on Earth today, and that the Earth exists solely for that purpose. Thus, each one of us should realize that our own decisions, actions, and, yes, even thoughts are of vital concern and will affect our lives greatly in the future, not only in this life, but in future lives as well. Remember the description of evolution, given in a reading, as being much like a brick wall being built one brick at a time. The evolution of the character of each soul's spirituality is determined by the sum total of all the decisions, thoughts, and actions it makes. Each one can be of great importance.

Whee; that lance is getting awfully heavy, but haven't we all had a good time jousting with the windmills of conventional thought. It is hoped the reader's mental juices have been stimulated, and will continue to flow after this book is put down. Now, go out and find your own windmills!

THE END

About the Author

Born and raised in Lexington, Kentucky, Bill received a Bachelor's Degree in Liberal Arts from the University of Kentucky before he and his wife moved to the Pacific Northwest. There, for 32 years, he divided his time between building airplanes, building houses, and helping his wife raise three children. The last ten years have seen he and his wife dividing their time between Puget Sound country and the Colorado River in Arizona. *Hindsight* is Bill's first literary effort but he hopes not the last.